Original German Publisher Information:

Author
Ingrid Perra

Editorial Office
Claudia Schmidt

Specialist Proofreading
Monika Behrend

Editing
Angelika Klein

Photographs
UZwei, Uli Glasemann

Styling
Elke Reith

Cover Design
Yvonne Rangnitt

Layout and Typesetting
GrafikwerkFreiburg

Technical Illustrations
Claudia Schmidt, Gabriela Reuß (p. 8 - 15)

Reproduction
Meyle + Müller, Pforzheim

Printing and Processing
Himmer AG, Augsburg

ISBN 978-3-8410-6002-0
Art.-Nr. OZ6002

© 2010
Christophorus Verlag
GmbH & Co. KG, Freiburg
All rights reserved.

Fabrics / Interfacing:
Freudenberg Vliesstoffe KG, Heidelberg
www.vlieseline.de

KnorrPrandell GmbH, Lichtenfels
www.knorrprandel.com

Stof A/S, Herning (DK)
www.stof-dk.com

Westfalenstoffe AG, Münster
www.westfalenstoffe.de

Accessories:
Gütermann AG, Gutach-Breisgau
www.guetermann.com

Prym Consumer Gmbh, Stolberg
www.prym-consumer.com

Rayher Hobby GmbH, Laupheim
www.rayher-hobby.de

Rinske Stevens Design, Culemborg (NL)
www.rinskestevensdesign.com

All models, illustrations, and photographs are copyrighted. Commercial use is prohibited. This also applies to reproduction and respectively distribution by electronic media.

The author and publisher have exercised the greatest possible care to ensure that all information and instructions are correct. However, in the case of incorrect information, the author and publisher can assume no liability at all for potential direct or indirect consequences.

The materials displayed are temporally without guarantee. The publisher does not assume responsibility and liability for availability and deliverability. The color and brightness of the threads, materials, and models displayed in this book can vary from the originals. The pictorial representation is without guarantee. The publisher does not assume responsibility or liability.

OZ creativ

Originally Titled: *Zauberhafte Weihnachtszeit: Kleine und große Patchworkideen für Winter & Advent*
Translated into English by: Christine Marie Elliston

Schiffer Books are available at special discounts for bulk purchases for sales promotions or premiums. Special editions, including personalized covers, corporate imprints, and excerpts can be created in large quantities for special needs. For more information contact the publisher.

Published by Schiffer Publishing, Ltd.
4880 Lower Valley Road
Atglen, PA 19310
Phone: (610) 593-1777; Fax: (610) 593-2002
E-mail: Info@schifferbooks.com

Other Schiffer Books on Related Subjects:
New Quilts. Nancy Rae. ISBN: 0887401570. $14.95

Library of Congress Control Number: 2012939907

Designed by Mark David Bowyer
Type set in MetaCondMediumLF / Frutiger T1

ISBN: 978-0-7643-4219-6
Printed in China

For the largest selection of fine reference books on this and related subjects, please visit our website at
www.schifferbooks.com
You may also write for a free catalog.

This book may be purchased from the publisher.
Please try your bookstore first.

We are always looking for people to write books on new and related subjects. If you have an idea for a book, please contact us at
proposals@schifferbooks.com

In Europe, Schiffer books are distributed by
Bushwood Books
6 Marksbury Ave.
Kew Gardens
Surrey TW9 4JF England
Phone: 44 (0) 20 8392 8585; Fax: 44 (0) 20 8392 9876
E-mail: info@bushwoodbooks.co.uk
Website: www.bushwoodbooks.co.uk

Ingrid Perra

Christmas Magic

Decorative Ideas
for Winter & Yuletide Patchwork

4880 Lower Valley Road • Atglen, PA 19310

Dear readers,

Ingrid Perra has turned her hobby into a business and established Country Quilt, a patchwork company, in Oberhausen. The name says it all; her concentration is in American country style. She is a course instructor and regularly publishes models in different patchwork trade journals.

The anticipation of the most beautiful time of year—advent and Christmas time—inspires us each year to decorate our homes in this spirit. We experience a special enjoyment when we create our own decorations. Placemats, pillows, cuddly blankets, and simple decorative pieces made with the right materials make an impact.

This book includes simple, stitched projects for beginners. Those more advanced may also find challenges reworking the complex patchwork. Let yourself be inspired by the big and small projects that I present you in this book. Whether you are initially selecting a simple model and would like to make your home cozy with a cuddly blanket or choose a more complex work and decorate your windowsill with a draft stopper—coordinate your design with your own home. The "advent house" is an extraordinary advent calendar for which you will receive great recognition. The step-by-step directions and mostly original size templates will make reworking the projects easy for you.

I wish you pleasant hours, much joy, and success with the realization of your projects.

Yours,

Ingrid Perra

Contents

Material

For patchwork and quilt work there are a few supplies that you will need. Here is a list of appropriate accessories:

1. Fabric

First, you will naturally need different fabrics. The exact types of fabric will be specified in the respective instructions. Because some fabrics, especially the vibrant colors, may change color and shrink a little, you should wash all fabrics, at the very least the cotton fabrics, before cutting, and separate the dark and light colors. Nearly all patchwork fabrics are available in a width of 45" [115 cm], some fabrics in a width of 55" or 59" [140 or 150 cm], the backing fabrics up to a width of 95" [240 cm]. When using the fabric you should certainly note that you may lose several inches from shrinkage after washing, and therefore it is preferable to purchase a little more rather than too little.

2. Cutting tools

You can cut single patchwork shapes either with scissors or a rotary cutter, which is more precise and faster by hand. The rotary cutter comes in different sizes (a small size is especially suited for curves) and is also available with interchangeable blades with different edges. If you are working with a rotary cutter you will also need a cutting mat, which is commercially available in different sizes.

3. Rulers

To make accurate cuts with a rotary cutter, the fabric is positioned onto a universal ruler. Then you can make precise cuts along the ruler edge. Also, with this ruler you can take readings of 30, 45, 60, and 90 degree angles, which you will need for cutting in many patchwork projects.

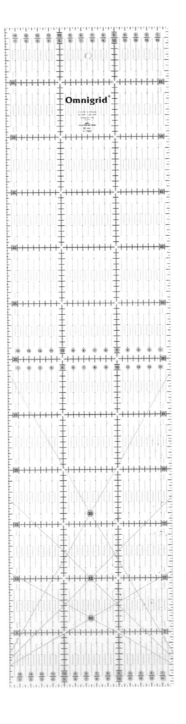

4. Copy paper

With copy paper you can spare yourself from transferring the templates first to tissue paper. Place the cardboard and the copy paper under the corresponding patterns of the work sheet and retrace the templates with a cutting wheel. Then the corresponding template is immediately visible on the cardboard or template sheet. Finally, cut out the templates.

5. Cardboard or template sheet for preparing templates

To copy the corresponding patchwork shapes onto templates, you will need a piece of cardboard or template sheet. First, the patterns from the work sheet are traced onto copy paper or tissue paper and then transferred onto the cardboard or the template sheet. If you need to prepare a triangle template, you can draw this with the corresponding measurements directly onto the cardboard or the template sheet. Finally, cut out the templates.

6. Freezer paper or Totally Stable

Templates made from freezer paper or Totally Stable can be used multiple times. They are fusible on one side, but they do not permanently adhere. After use they can be removed again without residue. If used carefully, you can use the templates 8 to 10 times.

7. Sewing thread and quilting thread

Cotton or polyester thread is used for sewing. For quilting there is a special quilting thread that is especially strong and waxed. In addition, there are special quilting threads, for example, invisible quilting thread or metallic quilting thread. There is a difference between machine and hand quilting thread.

8. Trick marker or silver marking pencil

To copy quilt motifs onto the fabric or additional lines or contours with appliqués, you will need special pens. If the marked lines must be invisible later, it is easiest to use a special trick marker that is water soluble (the lines disappear after washing) or fading (the lines vanish on their own after a while). If you use fading ink pens, only draw a few motifs beforehand that you can subsequently quilt. Otherwise, there is a chance that the lines could disappear before you finish the work.

Tip:

Do not press over these lines or else they can no longer be removed! If the marked lines should still be visible afterwards (which is advantageous with pretty quilt motifs) you should use a silver marking pencil especially with light, solid fabrics. It slightly shimmers through underneath the quilted lines afterwards. Of course, you can later remove the lines from the silver marking pencil with an eraser.

9. Pins

You will need many pins to put together the single patchwork pieces. For patching, use the extra long glass head pins and/or thin pins with flat heads.

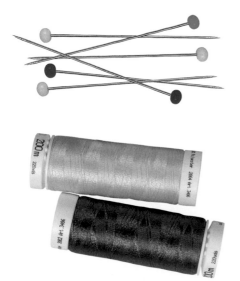

10. Brass safety pins (curved) or basting thread

To baste together the three layers (top, batting, and backing), you can either stitch together the three layers using large basting stitches or pin them together with large, curved safety pins.

11. Quilting needles

Special quilting needles, extra short and especially pointed, making quilting easier.

12. Quilting hoop and frame

So that the quilt pattern is especially beautiful and vivid, before quilting, the work is stretched in a quilting hoop or frame. Frames are available in oval, rectangular, and round shapes in different sizes and variations.

13. Thimble

You should absolutely use a thimble for quilting. Thimbles are available in metal or leather. The leather thimble is flexible and therefore fits all finger sizes and nail lengths. Also, for most patchworkers, working with a flexible thimble is easier than with an inflexible metal thimble. Simply see which thimble works better for you.

14. Machine quilting needles

If you would like to quilt with a sewing machine, you should use special machine quilting needles. These needles prevent the interfacing fabric from pulling up while quilting with a sewing machine.

15. Bias tape maker

With a bias tape maker, which is available in different widths, you can create a trim with which you can bind your work.

Tip!

Additionally, an iron and ironing board should always be readily available near the working area.

Basic Patchwork & Quilting Course

Precise measurement is a requirement for successful patchwork. Therefore, from the start make sure to accurately cut and sew together your individual patchwork pieces.

Preparations for your patchwork

After washing and sorting your fabrics, you can prepare the templates (see material on pages 6 - 7). For this, take the shape (here a triangle) from the original pattern with tissue paper and transfer onto a piece of template material, at the same time marking the fabric grain (see illustration).

Note!

Some patterns already have a seam allowance of 1/4" [0.75 cm], but for most the seam allowance must be added. However, this will always be specified.

Curved templates

With curved templates or shapes that are difficult to fit, it is advisable to mark on the seam allowances where small notches will be cut. If these notches are copied onto the fabric, the seams can be accurately sewn together (see illustrations below).

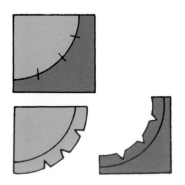

Cutting without templates

There is also a method of quickly and efficiently cutting squares, rectangles, and triangles without templates.
If you need many shapes from the same fabric, you can pile up the fabrics up to 4x. The shapes are then accurately cut out with the help of a rotary cutter, cutting mat, and universal ruler. You must note the following.

For squares and rectangles:

Cut the shapes with the corresponding measurement + 1/4" [0.75 cm] on all sides. The arrows mark the fabric grain.
In the instructions in this book the seam allowances are already included.

Final dimension
1/4" [0.75 cm] + 1/4" [0.75 cm] = 1/2" [1.5 cm]

1/4" [0.75 cm]   1/4" [0.75 cm]

Final dimension
1/4" [0.75 cm] + 1/4" [0.75 cm] = 1/2" [1.5 cm]

1/4" [0.75 cm]   1/4" [0.75 cm]

For right triangles whose short sides are on the straight of the grain:

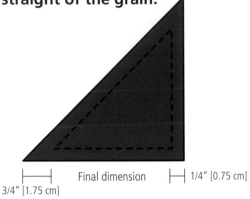

Final dimension   1/4" [0.75 cm]
3/4" [1.75 cm]

3/4" [1.75 cm] + 1/4" [0.75 cm] = 1" [2.5 cm]

With the help of cutting tools, see material on pages 6 - 7, you can cut all shapes for which no templates are necessary. For this purpose all specifications include a 1/4" [0.75 cm] seam allowance.

For these triangles, first cut out 1 square with the corresponding measurement + 1" [2.5 cm] seam allowance and cut through 1x on the diagonal. The arrows mark the fabric grain. This results in 2 triangles.

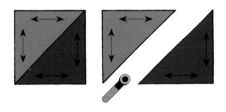

For these triangles first cut out 1 square with the corresponding measurement + 1 3/8" [3.5 cm] seam allowance and cut through 2x on the diagonal. The arrows mark the fabric grain. This results in 4 triangles.

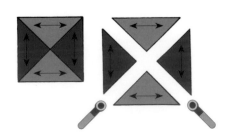

Sewing together

Place 1 pin at each acute angle corner and also distribute pins in between for large patchwork pieces.

By hand:

Sew together these seams with small running stitches according to the respective seam allowance and secure with a back stitch after every third running stitch.

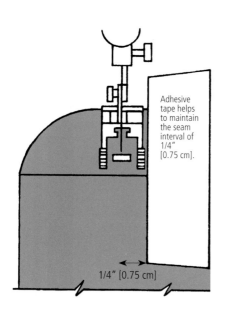

With a sewing machine:

Place 1 pin at each acute angle corner and also distribute pins in between for large patchwork pieces (just like sewing by hand). Then adjust the stitch length of the sewing machine. Apply adhesive tape on the sewing machine at an interval of 1/4″ [0.75 cm] from the seam line or use a correspondingly wide foot. On some sewing machines the position of the needle can be changed individually so that you maintain a 1/4″ [0.75 cm] wide seam allowance when you guide the fabric on the right side evenly under the sewing machine foot. The exact position of the needle must be tested each time.

Adhesive tape helps to maintain the seam interval of 1/4″ [0.75 cm].

1/4″ [0.75 cm]

Now sew together the pieces 1/4″ [0.75 cm] wide, at the same time removing the pins one after the other.

Chain stitch similar pieces together one after the other. This saves time and thread. Back stitches are not necessary at the seam ends.

Take the chain stitched pieces from the sewing machine and cut them apart.

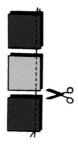

Joining the patchwork pieces

First, look closely at the patchwork block that is to be stitched or the edging: do all blocks or edging consist of the same shapes, or are triangles, squares, rectangles, etc., mixed? If triangles, squares, and rectangles are mixed, first sew together different triangles so that they form a square. Press the seams to one side and cut off the excess ends.

 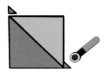

Stitch a square made from 2 or more triangles onto a simple square

or 2 squares next to each other

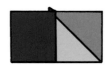

or squares, one below the other.

Sew together the squares that have been stitched together and the simple squares, one below the other, into rows,

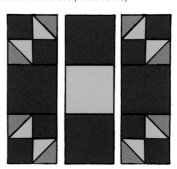

then the single rows into a block.

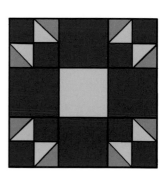

Of course you can first sew the squares together side by side into rows, then the rows, one below the other, into a block.

Pressing

Press the patchwork pieces from the right side as much as possible and always toward one side. The seams that are pressed to one side are more durable (the edges are not finished and hold the batting back). If possible, always press the seam allowances toward the darker side of the fabric so that no shadow is visible on the front side. The illustration shows 2 pieces that are sewn together and pressed to one side.

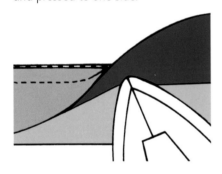

This is how the pressed seams look on the back side.

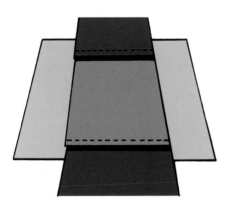

When two rows of joined patchwork pieces are stitched together, all seam allowances of the first row should be pressed in one direction, and those in the second row should be pressed in the opposite direction.

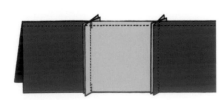

Thus, putting together the seams that meet at intersection points is much simpler, and the seams are not as thick. If more than two rows are sewn together, the 1st, 3rd, 5th, 7th, etc. rows are pressed in one direction, the 2nd, 4th, 6th, 8th, etc. are pressed in the opposite direction. The illustration below shows a perfectly pressed patchwork block from the back. At times it is unavoidable that some seam allowances are pressed behind the light fabric. You should accept this for the benefit of perfect intersection points.

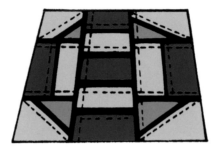

Pressing lengthwise strips:

Do not place the lengthwise strips on the ironing board horizontally,

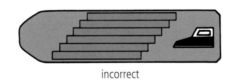

incorrect

but rather vertically.

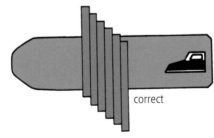

correct

In this way the strips are not pulled out of shape in one direction but are rather parallel.

Joining the layers

Cut the backing material approximately 2" [5 cm] larger than the patchwork top and lay flat onto the table—the right side facing down. Using adhesive tape fix the edges of the backing onto a base (table or floor). Place an equally large piece of volume fleece flat onto the backing. Put the patchwork piece on top with the right side facing up. Pin together the layers, always smoothing out the fabric by hand from the center toward the edges.

Using basting thread, stitch together the layers between the needles with large basting stitches; starting from the center first stitch diagonal, then horizontal, and vertical lines. At an approximate interval of 2" [5 cm] to 6" [15 cm] each make a basting line. After stitching, remove the pins.

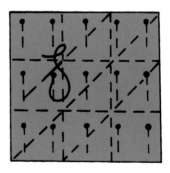

Tip!

Instead of using the method described above, you can also use curved safety pins (as many as possible). At the same time you will have pinned and stitched. However, you should note that during quilting (especially during machine quilting) the pins are very disruptive.

However the safety pins can gradually be removed during quilting, when they are no longer needed (for example, whenever a corresponding field is quilted). Try for yourself and see how you manage.

In the meantime there are also special basting guns or basting spray.

Quilting

Quilting serves to hold together the 3 layers (backing, batting, and patchwork top). In addition, the batting will not clump during washing. The different quilting patterns are additional decoration for the patchwork piece.

Quilting is always done from the center outward.

First you must trace the quilt motifs from the pattern. Adhere the motif onto a blank template sheet. Carefully cut out the lines of the motif, making sure that no loose parts are created so that the template remains as a whole. With a trick marker or silver marking pencil mark the lines through the pieces that are cut out and then join the potentially discontinuous lines.

Tip!

You can also buy finished templates for quilt motifs.

With motifs where only the edging is quilted, you can cut out the motif and directly transfer the outlines onto the fabric.

Tip!

The possibility also exists for you to mark the quilt motifs onto the fabric before joining the single layers (but not with the fading ink pen). When quilting a diagonal grid (for example, like with the placemats "eating in style") the lines are marked with a fading ink pen or chalk with the help of the 45° line of the cutting ruler.

Quilting by hand:

For quilting use a short quilting needle (for example, Between, size 9). Now stretch the quilt work in a quilting hoop or frame. Thread the quilting needle and tie a knot at the end of the thread. Put the needle into the fabric from the bottom at the desired location and pull the thread far enough so that the knot sticks in the filling. You can also put the needle into the fabric from the top side of the quilt and pull the knot into the filling. In doing so, firmly press the fabric on the needle entry point of the top side. Place a thimble on the middle finger of the hand used for sewing. Lay the eye against the thimble and bring the needle into the quilt so that the needle point meets the fingertip of your guiding hand under the quilt. Press against the quilt from the bottom with a finger on the other hand. If the needle point touches your finger under the quilt, bring it back to the top and pull the needle and thread through. You can protect your finger under the quilt with another thimble, preferably made of leather or plaster. Now quilt even running stitches through all three layers of the quilt.

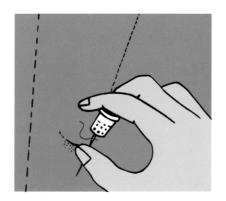

When you have more practice, you can take several stitches on a needle before you pull out the thread. The lines are then empirically nicer and straighter. Thus, you can quilt different patterns and lines. If you quilt along the seams or stitch in the ditch, this means that you quilt along the stitched line and on the side of the seam where the seam allowance is not located (otherwise during quilting you would have to quilt through 4 and not 2 layers of fabric).

Another possibility is to quilt 3/16" [5 mm] from both sides of the seam (see illustration).

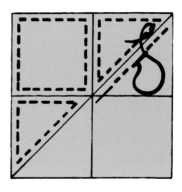

At the end of a quilting line wrap the thread 3x around the needle and bring it into the volume fleece. Guide the needle to the top again approximately 1" - 1 3/16" [2.5 cm - 3 cm] away and pull the thread so that the small knot slips under the fabric. If this is not comfortable for you because the thread is potentially too loose or pulled too tightly, you can use 2 - 3 back stitches on the line that is already quilted (but only through the top fabric layer) and pull the last end of the thread a bit through the filling, bring to the top again, and clip with some tension (so that the thread slides back into the filling).

Quilting by machine:

Use a 90 or special quilting needle in the sewing machine and slightly loosen the upper thread tension. Use the same thread strength for the upper and lower thread. You may want to use a special walking foot that many sewing machine companies offer and which joins the 3 layers without the individual fabrics puckering. You can apply a spacer for quilting parallel lines.

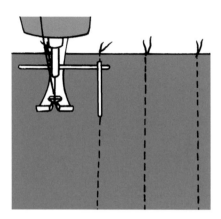

If you would like to quilt shapes freehand, use a darning foot or a quilting foot and lower the feed. Now quilt the surfaces freehand with wavy lines or other shapes, at the same time guiding the fabric with slow hand movements and a relatively higher sewing speed. The coordination of sewing speed and hand movement determines the stitch length. Here you should first practice on a sample in order to adjust to the speed and movement and also to coordinate the upper and lower thread tension.

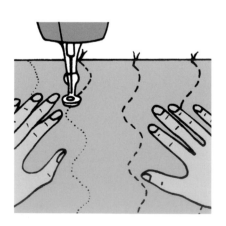

A quicker method is knotting:

This can be an interesting alternative. When putting together a quilt by knotting you should place a pin at each spot on which a knot will be included. Thread the needle with a long, strong thread (mercerized thread, crochet thread, or even matching wool). Sew 2 back stitches through all 3 layers at the same spot, while sewing over each pin. Keep the starting and ending threads approximately 2" - 3" [5 cm - 7.5 cm] long.

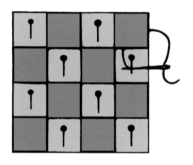

Knot together the thread ends flat, first right over left, then left over right. Pull the knots tight and cut off the ends to the same length.

Tip!

If the quilt is going to be washed a lot, it is recommended to incorporate as many knots as possible. Note that not every interfacing is suitable for knotting because it can shift out of place within the layers.

Stitching and turning with freezer paper

Copy the motif from the corresponding pattern onto the matte side of the freezer paper or Totally Stable™ with a pencil and cut out.

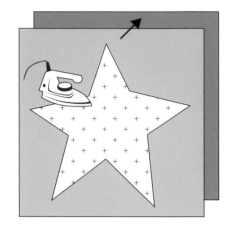

Press these templates onto the back of the appliqué fabric. Cut out the fabric freehand and lay onto another piece of fabric with the right sides together. Along the edge of the freezer paper sew together both layers all around with

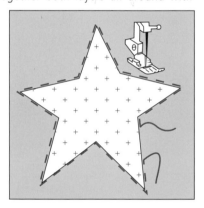

small stitches (1/32" - 1/16" [1 mm - 1.5 mm] stitch length), however, leave an opening for turning. Carefully pull off the freezer paper template (it can be re-used up to ten times).

Trim the seam allowances to 3/16" [5 mm]; with curves and points cut the seam allowances in the valleys and curves just before the seam.

Turn the piece, work out the seams. Fill the motif with synthetic stuffing, close the opening by hand.

Types of appliqué

Machine appliqué with satin stitch:

Transfer the pieces of the motif onto the paper side of the Vliesofix, cut out freehand, and press onto the back of the fabric; press from where the appliqué will be made. Cut out the motif exactly along the outline.

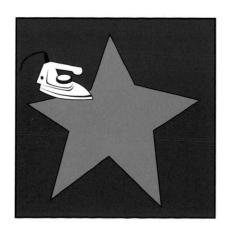

Now remove the remaining Vliesofix backing paper. Lay the piece onto the background fabric and check the precise location. As long as the Vliesofix has not been attached from pressing, the position of the motif can be adjusted at any time. Press. Place the motif freehand behind the background fabric with embroidery interfacing (puckering of the fabric is prevented).

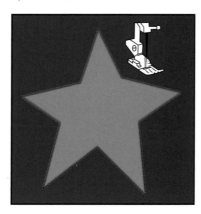

Appliqué with matching machine embroidery thread and compact zigzag stitching.

Tip!

Practice sewing on waste fabric beforehand, if necessary, adjust the stitch length and width. Try a stitch length of 0.2 mm - 0.3 mm [0.007" - 0.011"] and a width of 2 - 3.

Stitching and turning appliqué with freezer paper:

The stitched and turned appliqué is used to display motifs more vividly; each motif is stitched and turned before it's appliquéd.

Proceed in the same manner as was described under "stitching and turning with freezer paper."

However, now completely sew around the freezer paper template without leaving an opening for turning.

Trim the seam allowances to 3/16" [5 mm]; with curves and points cut the seam allowances in the valleys and curves just before the seam. On the back make a cut through the layer of fabric, turn the piece, work out the seams. The opening for turning is not closed again because it is hidden by appliquéing.

Sew the stitched and turned appliqué on the background with small hem stitching.

Tip!

Choose a thread color that matches the appliqué piece.

Proper finishing

After quilting, trim the backing and batting all around to the size of the front side. Now finish the entire work. The edging mostly has a binding that is coordinating or contrasting with the background fabric. The binding can consist of a finished or self-made bias strip (especially suitable for curves) or a corresponding binding (for straight pieces) on a straight grain. If the length of the fabric is not sufficient for the complete edging or a side of the patchwork, first different bias strips or straight strips must be made. In order for the strips to have a seam that is as even as possible when sewing together the individual strips that are cut on a straight grain, the narrow sides should be sewn together like the bias strip at a 45° angle (see below "making the bias strip"). The width of the seam allowance is 1/4" [0.75 cm]. The excess corners are cut off afterwards. Press the seam apart.

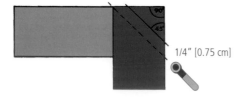

1/4" [0.75 cm]

For the binding (not to confuse with the edging of the center section), you have the following methods at your disposal:

Method 1 (each individual side):

First cut strips that are 2 1/2" [6.5 cm] each or at a width of the required length according to the information in the respective instructions and (if necessary) quilt together on each narrow side. Then press the binding on top of each other on the lengthwise sides with the reverse sides together. Pin the doubled binding with the open edges first on the two opposite sides of the front side with the right sides together and quilt. Press the binding halfway onto the backing and stitch by hand with small hem stitches. Proceed with the remaining binding on both other borders in the same fashion. However, before putting around the trim sew together the narrow sides or press them inward.

Method 2 (continuous binding):

First cut strips that are 2 1/2" [6.5 cm] or at a width of the required length according to the information in the respective instructions and quilt together on each narrow side, as was described.

Tip!

For each given length always add slightly more and trim the strips to the appropriate length before sewing together the start of the strips and the strip ends. Then press the strips on top of each other with the

reverse sides together. Lay the strip with the doubled open edges onto the front side of the quilt with the right sides together and pin up to the first corner, beginning on one middle side and not stitching down the first approximately 4" [10 cm] of the strip. Now pin the strip up to the first corner, ending 1/4" [0.75 cm] from the bottom border (= at the corner point) and secure the end of the seam.

Then turn the quilt 90 degrees into position for sewing the following side. First fold up the strip to create a 45 degree angle.

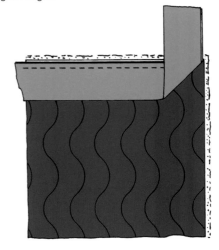

Fold it down again so that the edge of the strip is even on the top border. You may want to pin the edge.

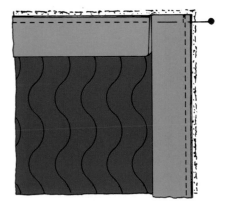

Now sew the strip on the following side, beginning with stitching directly on the top border and securing the beginning of the seam. Sew on the strip all around and proceed with the other three corners in the same way. At the end do not stitch down the last approximately 4" [10 cm]. Check the remaining required length and cut to size, not forgetting the seam allowances. Now sew together the beginning and end of the strip onto the narrow sides. Then stitch the remaining seam of the trim. Place the trim halfway onto the backing, forming a diagonal fold on each corner that corresponds to the fold that was formed on the front side. Lastly, stitch down the strip with small hem stitches by hand on the backing so that the seam is hidden. You may want to close the diagonal folds on the corners with several stitches by hand. The following illustration displays the finished binding.

Finishing without binding:

For many patchwork projects you do not need binding. With this method the 3 layers are only stitched and turned. First trim the backing and the batting to the size of the front side. Then position the front side and backing on top of each other with the right sides together, and apply the interfacing on the top, making sure that the 3 layers are nicely smoothed out and the outer edges are even. Now quilt all 3 layers along the outer edges, leaving a small opening for turning on one side. Finish the outer edges with narrow zigzag stitches or with an overlock sewing machine. Trim the seam allowances on the corners until shortly before the seam line. Turn the piece. Close the opening by hand. Now complete the stitching and quilt work.

Making the bias strip

Method 1:

First cut the strips on the bias. Then sew together these strips.

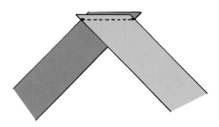

Cut 2 or more strips according to desired length, sew together, and trim to the corresponding length.

Method 2:

This method is especially recommended if you need very long bias strips. First cut a square that is approximately 20" x 20" [50 cm x 50 cm] or corresponds to the model instructions. Now cut through the square 1x on the diagonal so that 2 triangles are formed.

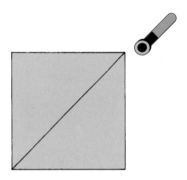

Then sew together both of these triangles. Press the seam apart. Then per the illustration mark lines at intervals of the width of the bias strip.

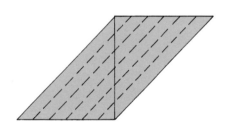

Now close this surface to form a tunnel, moving the pointed corners to the width of the strip so that the edge meets the first line that is to be cut.

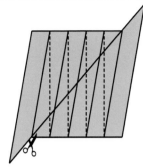

Press apart the seam. Then from the area corresponding to the marked lines cut a continuous strip to the desired length using scissors.

Size:
19 3/4" x 17 3/8"
[50 cm x 44 cm]
(incl. hanger)

Material

For the front side, the appliqués, and the binding:

Cotton fabrics, each approximately 43 1/4" [110 cm] wide:

 A = 13 3/4" x 17 3/4"
[35 cm x 45 cm]
Black with little stars

 B = 6" x 17 3/4"
[15 cm x 45 cm]
White with gold dots

 C = 6" x 21 5/8"
[15 cm x 55 cm]
White

 D = 10" x 43 1/4"
[25 cm x 110 cm]
Red striped pattern

 E = 2" x 9"
[5 cm x 22 cm]
Red-green-blue-yellow checkered pattern

 F = 2" x 6"
[5 cm x 15 cm]
Red dotted pattern

 G = 4" x 43 1/4"
[10 cm x 110 cm]
Green dotted pattern

 H = 4" x 43 1/4"
[10 cm x 110 cm]
Green

 I = 6" x 43 1/4"
[15 cm x 110 cm]
Yellow with stars

 K = 6" x 43 1/4"
[15 cm x 110 cm]
Yellow dotted pattern

For the backing:

C = 15 3/4" x 20"
[40 cm x 50 cm]

Materials continued on page 18

Snow Gently Falls

These snowmen and small Christmas trees create a joyful winter atmosphere in the home. All motifs on this wall hanging are made according to the method "stitching and turning with freezer paper." Using this type of appliqué, the pieces appear especially vivid and lively.

A jolly winter wall hanging

Preparation

You will find the templates on pages 80 – 82. They do not include seam allowances. The letters indicate the fabric that is to be used. Copy the outline of the snowmen, hats, and tree sections from the pattern onto freezer paper and cut out accurately.

Cutting

Measurements include 1/4" [0.75 cm] seam allowances.

For the front side

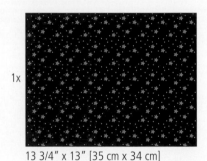
1x
13 3/4" x 13" [35 cm x 34 cm]

1x
6" x 13" [15 cm x 34 cm]

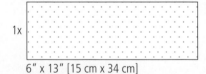
2x
2" x 11" [5.5 cm x 28.5 cm]

2x
2" x 19 1/2" [5.5 cm x 49.5 cm]

For the appliqués

1x
1 3/8" x 9" [3.5 cm x 22 cm]

1x
1 3/8" x 10" [3.5 cm x 25 cm]

For the backing

1x
15 3/4" x 20" [40 cm x 50 cm]

For the batting

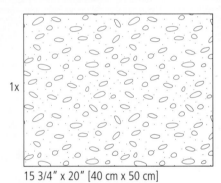
1x
15 3/4" x 20" [40 cm x 50 cm]

For the binding

2x
2 1/2" x 43 1/4" [6.5 cm x 110 cm]

For the batting:

 17 3/4" x 29 1/2"
[45 cm x 75 cm]
Volume Fleece
Freudenberg HH 650

Additional supplies:

15 3/4" x 15"
[40 cm x 38 cm]
Freezer paper

- 4 small, black buttons (snowmen eyes)
- Motif buttons for embellishment: 3 heart-shaped buttons (large snowman), 3 small, round buttons (small snowman), 11 small, star-shaped buttons (trees), 2 large motif buttons for the wreaths (treetop)
- Black and red embroidery thread
- Matching sewing and quilting thread
- 1 wooden rod, dia. 25/64" [10 mm], 20" [50 cm] long

Piecing

Center section

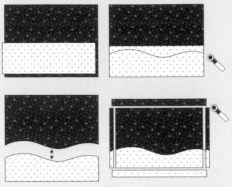

Lay the rectangle made from fabric B ⬜ onto the bottom lengthwise edge of the rectangle made from fabric A ⬛ with the reverse side on the right side. Copy the outline of the wavy cut and cut through both layers of fabric with a rotary cutter. Sew together the bottom cut from fabric B ⬜ and the top cut from fabric A. ⬛ The remaining fabric is no longer needed. Trim the newly formed rectangle to a size of 16 5/16" x 11 1/4" [41.5 cm x 28.5 cm].

Edging

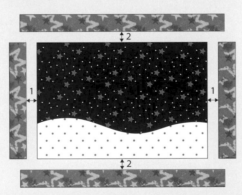

Border the center section with the strips made from fabric I. ▣ First sew on the shorter strips on the left and right, then the longer strips on the top and bottom.

Appliqués

Snowmen scarves

Position the strips made from fabrics D ▥ and E ▦ lengthwise with the right sides together for the snowmen scarves and sew together foot-wide on the open edges, leaving a 2" [5 cm] opening for turning. Turn the pieces, and close the opening by hand.

Snowmen

The snowmen are made according to the method "stitching and turning appliqué with freezer paper" (see basic course on page 13), additionally volume fleece HH 650 is sewn in.

On the back side make a 3/4" - 1" [2 cm - 3 cm] cut, turn the pieces, work out the seams, close the opening by hand. Sew the motifs by hand with matching thread onto the background. First sew on the bodies of the snowmen then the small buttons for the eyes. Embroider the mouth with black twist embroidery thread and the nose with red twist embroidery thread. Bring each scarf behind the body and tie to the side after sewing on. Sew on the hat and cap.

Trees

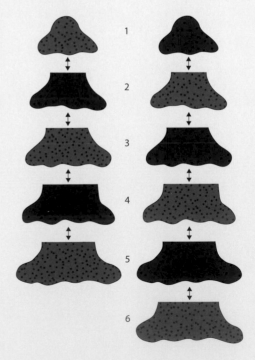

The trees are also made according to the method "stitching and turning appliqué with freezer paper" (on p. 12). However, here the straight top edge can remain open for turning because the sections of the tree are positioned on top of each other. The exception is the topmost piece; work it with an opening for turning here on the back side. Layer the pieces, overlapping approximately 3/8" [1 cm] (starting at the bottom), and sew by hand.

For the small tree make a total of 5 sections. Alternate between piece 1 made from fabric G ▨, piece 2 made from fabric H, ▨ etc. For the large tree 6 sections are necessary. The first section begins with fabric H ▧.

Sew on the star-shaped and wreath buttons.

Joining the layers

Place the front side (top), interfacing, and backing fabric on top of each other, the right fabric sides of the front side and backing should face outward. Trim the backing fabric and interfacing to the size of the front side. Press all three layers with steam.

Quilting

Quilt all stitched strips in the ditch.

Hanger

For the hanger, make the moon and stars out of fabric K according to the method "stitching and turning with freezer paper" (see basic course on page 12), however, additionally include HH 650 for each one. Make the moon 2x, the stars 6x, making sure that you cut half of the templates inversely because they are not symmetric. Place each two inverse pieces on top of each other and sew together at certain points on the left and right (see the markings on the original size template).

Finishing

Apply the continuous binding by sewing together the 2 strips made from fabric D ▥ on the short sides. Proceed as is described in the basic course on page 14.

Sew on the bottom edges of the moon and the points of the stars by hand on the top border of the wall hanging. Insert a wooden rod through the loops that were created by the moon and stars.

Size:
4" x 8"
[10 cm x 20 cm]
4 3/8" x 9"
[11 cm x 22 cm]
(incl. stand)

Material
For 2 trees

Cotton fabrics
Approximately 43 1/4" [110 cm] wide:

 G = 8" x 43 1/4"
[20 cm x 110 cm]
Green dotted pattern

 H = 8" x 43 1/4"
[20 cm x 110 cm]
Green

 L = 4" x 21 5/8"
[10 cm x 55 cm]
Green with large white dots

Additional supplies:

8" x 15" [20 cm x 38 cm] freezer paper

• Synthetic stuffing
• 10 small red, white, and natural-colored star-shaped buttons
• 2 wooden Tilda figure stands

Small Christmas tree stand up display

Preparation

You will find the templates on page 82. They do not include seam allowances. Make preparations, as was described with the wall hanging.

Piecing

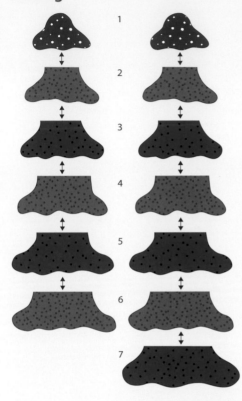

The trees are made like the trees on the wall hanging. However, make sure that during sewing that the tree sections on the straight top edges remain open, as well as the openings on the bottom wavy border. Secure the beginning and end of the seam.

The small tree consists of 6 sections. The large tree is made up of 7 sections. Section 1 (the top) is sewn with fabric **L** ▨, then alternate between fabrics **G** ▨ and **H** ▪. Turn the individual sections after sewing together, work out the seams and tips.

Finishing

Fit the sections into each other approximately 3/8" [1 cm] each for the large and small tree, turn the seam allowances 1/4" [0.75 cm] inward within the area of the wavy opening, sew together the crossing seams by hand. Gently fill the trees with stuffing. Sew on the buttons. Close the bottom opening of both trees except for 3/8" [1 cm], and insert the rod of the wooden stand here.

North Star

Red and white—the Nordic colors that conjure a festive spirit on the table, the ornaments decorate the Christmas tree branch, the cabinet, or the door knob. On the matching chalkboard with the Christmas elf you can bid visitors welcome.

Nordic tablecloth

Material

For the front side and the binding:

Cotton fabrics, approximately 59" [150 cm wide]:

A = 31 1/2" x 59"
[80 cm x 150 cm]
White with red dots

B = 20" x 59"
[50 cm x 150 cm]
Red

C = 15 3/4" x 59"
[40 cm x 150 cm]
Natural-red checkered pattern

D = 11 3/4" x 43 1/4"
[30 cm x 110 cm]
Natural-red diagonal checkered pattern

For the backing:

E = 47 1/4" x 47 1/4"
[120 cm x 120 cm]
Natural-colored

For the batting:

47 1/4" x 47 1/4"
[120 cm x 120 cm]
Volume Fleece
Freudenberg 249

Additional supplies:
• Matching sewing and quilting thread

Cutting

Measurements include 1/4" [0.75 cm] seam allowances.

For the center section

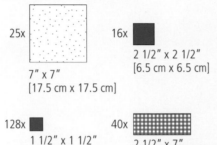

25x   7" x 7"
[17.5 cm x 17.5 cm]

16x   2 1/2" x 2 1/2"
[6.5 cm x 6.5 cm]

128x   1 1/2" x 1 1/2"
[4 cm x 4 cm]

40x   2 1/2" x 7"
[6.5 cm x 17.5 cm]

For the edging

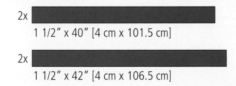

2x   1 1/2" x 40" [4 cm x 101.5 cm]

2x   1 1/2" x 42" [4 cm x 106.5 cm]

For the backing

1x

47 1/4" x 47 1/4" [120 cm x 120 cm]

For the batting

1x

47 1/4" x 47 1/4" [120 cm x 120 cm]

For the binding

1x

2 1/2" x 43 1/4" [6.5 cm x 110 cm]

Piecing
Sashing with Connector Corners

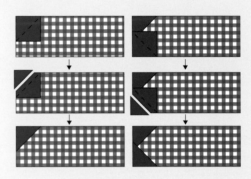

The rectangles made from fabric C ▦ are provided with connector corners. For this, mark a center diagonal on the reverse side of the fabric of each 1 1/2" x 1 1/2" [4 cm x 4 cm] square made from fabric B ■. Pin the square onto an outer edge of the rectangle made from fabric C ▦ with the right sides together and sew the diagonal. Cut off an approximately 1/4" [0.75 cm] wide seam allowance measured from the seam, fold back the triangle, and press. On the opposite side sew on a square made from fabric C ▦ in the same way.

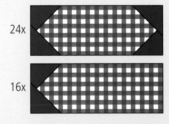

24x

16x

Twenty-four rectangles are provided with two connector corners each on both ends, sixteen rectangles only on one side.

Center section

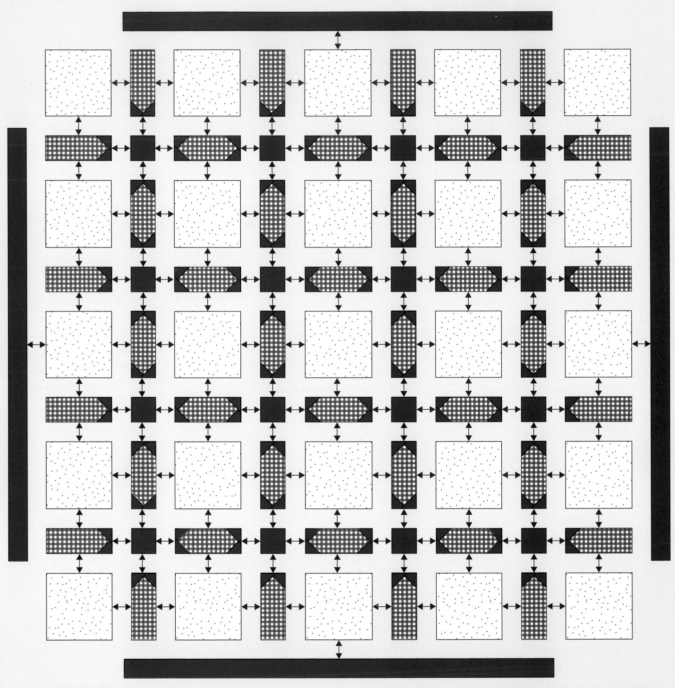

Lay out the completed strips with connector corners and the squares made from fabrics **A** ▫ and **B** ■ according to the schematic drawing and join into rows.

When pressing, make sure that the seam allowances of the rows alternately point in different directions. Sew together the rows, making sure that the seam points cross.

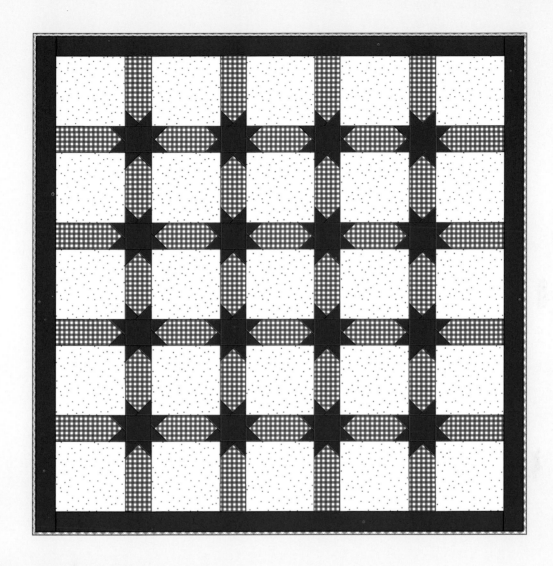

Edging

Border the center section with strips made from fabric **B** ■.

Joining the layers

Baste the front side onto the volume fleece and backing fabric (see basic course on page 10).

Quilting

Quilt the blocks in the ditch.

Finishing

Trim the interfacing and backing to the size of the front side. Apply the continuous binding, sewing together the 4 strips made from fabric **D** ⊠ on the short sides. Continue as described in the basic course on page 14.

Size of the ornaments
5 1/2" x 5 1/2"
[14 cm x 14 cm]
(without hangers)

Material

for 6 ornaments

For the front sides and backing:

Cotton fabrics, each approximately 59" or 43 1/4" [150 cm or 110 cm] wide:

 A = 8" x 59"
[20 cm x 150 cm]
White with red dots

 B = 8" x 59"
[20 cm x 150 cm]
Red

 C = 4" x 59"
[10 cm x 150 cm]
Natural-red checkered pattern

 D = 4" x 43 1/4"
[10 cm x 110 cm]
Red with white dots

For the batting:

 8" x 59"
[20 cm x 150 cm]
Volume Fleece
Freudenberg HH 650

Ornaments

Cutting

Measurements include 1/4" [0.75 cm] seam allowances.

Ornament 1 (block with star: red star, dotted border)

For the front side

1x ▪ 2 1/2" x 2 1/2"
[6.5 cm x 6.5 cm]

8x ▪ 1 1/2" x 1 1/2"
[4 cm x 4 cm]

4x ▦ 1 1/2" x 2 1/2"
[4 cm x 6.5 cm]

4x ▦ 1 1/2" x 1 1/2"
[4 cm x 4 cm]

2x ▭ 1 3/8" x 4 3/8"
[3.5 cm x 11 cm]

2x ▭ 1 3/8" x 6"
[3.5 cm x 15.5 cm]

For the backing

1x 6" x 6"
[15.5 cm x 15.5 cm]

For the hanger

1x 1 1/2" x 5 7/8"
[4 cm x 15 cm]

Ornament 2 (block with star: red star, checkered border)

For the front side

4x ▭ 1 1/2" x 2 1/2"
[4 cm x 6.5 cm]

4x ▫ 1 1/2" x 1 1/2"
[4 cm x 4 cm]

1x ▪ 2 1/2" x 2 1/2"
[6.5 cm x 6.5 cm]

8x ▪ 1 1/2" x 1 1/2"
[4 cm x 4 cm]

2x ▦ 1 3/8" x 4 1/2"
[3.5 cm x 11.5 cm]

2x ▦ 1 3/8" x 6"
[3.5 cm x 15.5 cm]

For the backing

1x 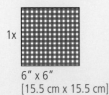 6" x 6"
[15.5 cm x 15.5 cm]

For the hanger

1x 1 1/2" x 5 7/8"
[4 cm x 15 cm]

Ornament 3 (block: square within a square with red border)

For the front side

1x  2 1/2" x 2 1/2"
[6.5 cm x 6.5 cm]

2x 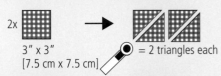 = 2 triangles each
2 3/8" x 2 3/8"
[6 cm x 6 cm]

2x 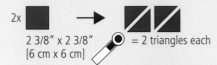 = 2 triangles each
3" x 3"
[7.5 cm x 7.5 cm]

2x  1 3/8" x 4 1/2"
[3.5 cm x 11.5 cm]

2x 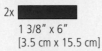 1 3/8" x 6"
[3.5 cm x 15.5 cm]

For the backing

1x 6" x 6"
[15.5 cm x 15.5 cm]

For the hanger

1x 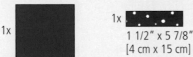 1 1/2" x 5 7/8"
[4 cm x 15 cm]

Ornament 4 (block: square within a square with checkered border)

For the front side

1x ▦ 2 1/2" x 2 1/2"
[6.5 cm x 6.5 cm]

2x 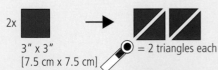 = 2 triangles each
2 3/8" x 2 3/8"
[6 cm x 6 cm]

2x 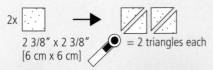 = 2 triangles each
3" x 3"
[7.5 cm x 7.5 cm]

2x 1 3/8" x 4 1/2"
[3.5 cm x 11.5 cm]

2x  1 3/8" x 6"
[3.5 cm x 15.5 cm]

For the backing

1x 6" x 6"
[15.5 cm x 15.5 cm]

For the hanger

1x 1 1/2" x 6"
[4 cm x 15.5 cm]

Ornament 5 (nine-patch block with red border)

For the front side

4x ◻ 1 3/4" x 1 3/4"
[4.5 cm x 4.5 cm]

1x ◼ 1 3/4" x 1 3/4"
[4.5 cm x 4.5 cm]

4x ▦ 1 3/4" x 1 3/4"
[4.5 cm x 4.5 cm]

2x ▬ 1 1/2" x 4 1/8"
[4 cm x 10.5 cm]

2x ▬ 1 1/2" x 6"
[4 cm x 15.5 cm]

For the backing

1x ◼ 6" x 6"
[15.5 cm x 15.5 cm]

For the hanger

1x ▬ 1 1/2" x 5 7/8"
[4 cm x 15 cm]

Ornament 6 (nine-patch block with white dotted border)

For the front side

1x ◻ 1 3/4" x 1 3/4"
[4.5 cm x 4.5 cm]

4x ◼ 1 3/4" x 1 3/4"
[4.5 cm x 4.5 cm]

4x ▦ 1 3/4" x 1 3/4"
[4.5 cm x 4.5 cm]

2x ▬ 1 1/2" x 4 1/8"
[4 cm x 10.5 cm]

2x ▬ 1 1/2" x 6"
[4 cm x 15.5 cm]

For the backing

1x ◻ 6" x 6"
[15.5 cm x 15.5 cm]

For the hanger

1x ▬ 1 1/2" x 5 7/8"
[4 cm x 15 cm]

Piecing

Ornament 1

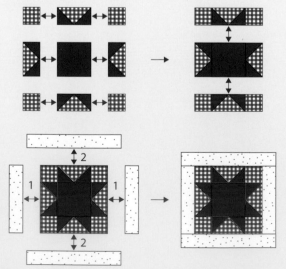

Ornament 2

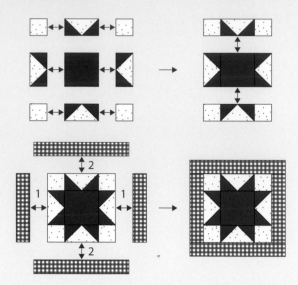

Sew on the squares for the connector corners onto the rectangles, as is described with the tablecloth. Lay out all pieces as is shown in the illustration.

First sew together the pieces into rows, then piece together the rows one underneath the other. Make sure that the seam allowances of the rows alternately face different directions. On the center section first sew on the border strips on the left and right, then on the top and bottom.

Ornament 3

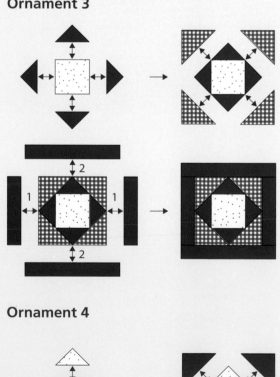

Ornament 4

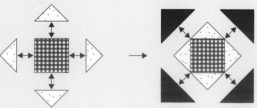

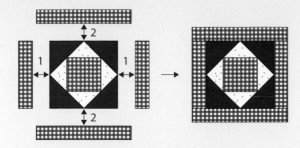

Sew two of the smaller triangles onto the left and right sides of the 2 3/8" x 2 3/8" [6 cm x 6 cm] center square, fold back, and press. Then sew on the remaining two smaller triangles onto the top and bottom, fold back, and press. Apply the larger triangles onto the resulting square in the same way. Sew the border strips on the center section first on the left and right, then the top and bottom.

Ornament 5

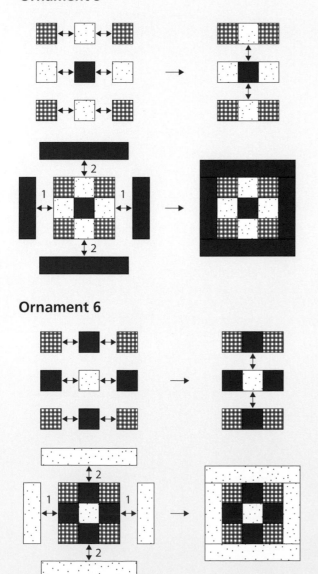

Ornament 6

Lay out the squares as is shown in the illustration and sew together into rows. Make sure that the seam allowances of the rows alternately face different directions. Piece together the rows, making sure that the seam points accurately intersect. On the center section first sew the border strips on the left and right, then on the top and bottom.

Ornaments 1 to 6

With the right sides together, baste all 6 pieces first onto the respective backing square and then onto the correspondingly large piece of volume fleece all around—except for an approximately 2" [5 cm] opening for turning—sew together foot-wide, turn the pieces, close the opening by hand. Press the pieces.

Quilting

Quilt in the ditch.

Finishing

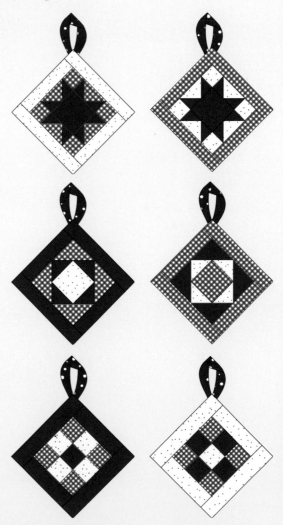

Fold the strips for the hangers lengthwise toward the center with the reverse sides together and press. Fold back and fold each lengthwise edge once again toward the center. Tuck in the short ends 3/8" [1 cm] each and press all 4 layers. 3/8" x 5" [1 cm x 13 cm] finished strips are made. Quilt the strips close to the edge, position toward the hanger, and on a corner of the ornament sew on the backing by hand.

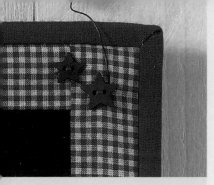

Size:
9 5/8" x 12 3/8"
[24.5 cm x 31.5 cm]

Material

For the board:

Cotton fabrics, each approximately 59" [150 cm] wide:

 A = 8" x 11 3/4" [20 cm x 30 cm] Black chalkboard sheet or artificial leather

For the front side and binding:

Cotton fabrics, each approximately 43 1/4" [110 cm] wide:

 B = 4" x 59" [10 cm x 150 cm] Natural-red checkered pattern

 C = 4" x 59" [10 cm x 150 cm] Red

For the backing:

 D = 13 3/4" x 21 5/8" [35 cm x 55 cm] Red

For the batting:

 10" x 13 3/4" [25 cm x 35 cm] Thermolam

For the stabilization:

 8" x 11 3/8" [20 cm x 29 cm] cardboard

Additional supplies:
• 3 1/4' [1 m] black florist's wire
• 3 red star-shaped buttons

Elf Chalkboard

Cutting

Measurements include 1/4" [0.75 cm] seam allowances

For the front side

1x
7" x 10" [18 cm x 25 cm]

1x
1 3/4" x 59" [4.5 cm x 150 cm]

For the backing

1x
9 5/8" x 12 3/8" [24.5 cm x 31.5 cm] (back side)

1x
9" x 12 3/8" [22.5 cm x 31.5 cm] (pocket)

For the binding

1x
2 1/2" x 59" [6.5 cm x 150 cm]

Piecing

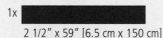
---- = Quilting line

Border the chalkboard sheet with the strips made from fabric **B** ⊞ in clockwise direction; the first strip is sewn onto the left, then the top, right, and bottom. To protect the sheet during pressing, use a pressing cloth. Pin the finished front piece onto a correspondingly large piece of Thermolam and backing fabric.

Quilting

Quilt in the ditch between the sheet and border. After quilting, trim the backing and batting to the size of the front side.

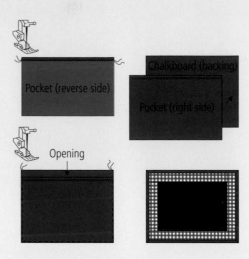

For the back pocket, in which later the cardboard will be inserted for stabilization, tuck in the rectangle made from the backing fabric 3/8" [1 cm] on a long side, which will later form the top border, and finish with zigzag stitching. Lay out the pocket piece on the backing even with the edges (left, right, and bottom) and quilt close to the edge (not foot-wide) on these 3 sides. This stitching prevents the pocket from shifting out of place.

Finishing

Sew on the strips for the binding all around as is described in the basic course on page 14 (continuous binding). Insert the cardboard into the back pocket.

Sew 3 star-shaped buttons on the left and right edging of the front piece. Wind the wire around a pencil, pull off, and carefully stretch to a length of 20" [50 cm], and wrap the end pieces around the buttons on the top chalkboard border. An option is to attach a small bow made from leftover fabric onto the wire.

Size:
9" x 4"
[23 cm x 10 cm]

Material

For the elf:

Cotton fabrics
Approximately 43 1/4" [110 cm] wide:

 A = 6" x 43 1/4"
[15 cm x 110 cm]
Natural-colored

 B = 4" x 10" [10 cm x
25 cm] Natural-red
checkered pattern

 C = 4" x 21 5/8"
[10 cm x 55 cm]
Red

 D = 2" x 10"
[5 cm x 25 cm] Black

Additional supplies:

 4" x 15" [10 cm x 38 cm]
Freezer paper

 1/2" x 10" [1.5 cm x 25 cm]
Black felt

• 10" [25 cm] natural-colored rick rack
• 1 packet light, natural-colored Tilda hair
• 2 star-shaped buttons
• 2 small, red buttons
• Synthetic stuffing
• Black twist embroidery thread
• 19 3/4" [50 cm] natural-colored cord
• 2 pieces 3/4" x 3/4" x 1 1/2" [2 cm x 2 cm x 4 cm] sponge

Elf

Preparation

You will find the templates on page 84. They do not include seam allowances.

Copy the patterns for the body, dress, cap, arms, and legs onto freezer paper and cut out accurately. Cut out the patterns for the arms and legs two times. Also copy the letters for the corresponding fabrics and the markings for the openings for turning. The lines for the seams of the set of strips are also marked on the templates. Transfer these, as well, and align on the seams of the set of strips.

Cutting

Measurements include 1/4" [0.75 cm] seam allowances

For the set of strips for the arms

1x   1 7/8" x 4 3/4"
[4.75 cm x 12 cm]

1x   4 3/8" x 4 3/4"
[8.75 cm x 12 cm]

For the set of strips for the legs

1x   2 1/4" x 11 3/4" [5.75 cm x 30 cm]

1x   4 3/8" x 11 3/4" [8.75 cm x 30 cm]

Piecing

Strip sets for the arms   Strip sets for the legs

1 1/2" [4 cm]   3" [8 cm]   2" [5 cm]   3" [8cm]

4 3/4" [12 cm]   11 3/4" [30 cm]

For the arms make a set of strips from fabrics **A** ■ and **B** ▦ , for the legs a set of strips out of fabrics **A** ■ and **D** ▦ . Fold both sets of strips lengthwise with the right sides together so that the seams lay exactly on top of each other.

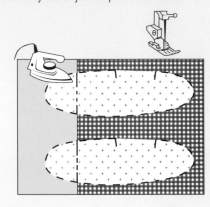

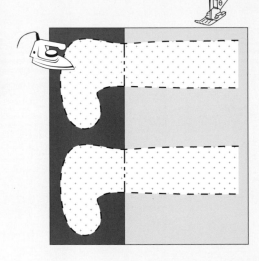

Press 2 freezer paper templates of the templates B (arms) and C (legs) with enough space for the seam allowances onto an outside left fabric side of the respective set of strips. Make sure that the lines marked on the templates lie on the seams of the set of strips. Sew together both layers of fabric along the freezer paper edge all around except for an opening for turning (1/32" - 1/16" [1 mm - 1.5 mm] stitch length), cut out pieces with a 3/16" [0.5 cm] seam allowance, remove the freezer paper, turn, and fill gently with stuffing. Close the opening by hand.

Press template A (body) onto fabric **A** ■ , laying a correspondingly large piece of fabric underneath.

Sew together the body on both sides and on top, cut out with a 1 cm seam allowance, cut the seam allowances in the curves, remove the freezer paper, and turn the piece. Turn the bottom edge 3/8" [1 cm] inward and press. Fill the body with stuffing, insert the legs on the lower border, and quilt close to the edge.

For the dress, cut 2 pieces according to template D, however, add a 1/4" [0.75 cm] seam allowance on each side and a 3/8" [1 cm] seam allowance on the top and bottom border. Sew together at the sides. Turn the top and bottom border 3/16" [0.5 cm] inward each 2 times and quilt, and sew on rick rack at the hem. Sew on two natural-colored, star-shaped buttons on the front side.

For the cap, cut a piece according to template E plus a 1/4" [0.75 cm] seam allowance and sew together at the angled sides with the right sides together. Turn the piece. Fold the border of the cap 3/8" [1 c(253) m] inward, fill the cap with stuffing.

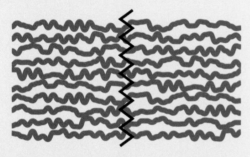

For the hair cut 10 pieces of wool that are approximately 8" [20 cm] long and lay out next to each other. In the center sew together the wool threads with the zigzag stitch on the sewing machine. Pull the hair over the head and attach with several stitches. Put on the cap and sew onto the head by hand. If you like, shorten the hair to the desired length.

Finishing

Embroider the eyes and mouth with twist embroidery thread.

Pull the dress over the body. Sew on the arms by means of the small red buttons. Tie around the felt scarf. Pull the cord with a darning needle through the hand and knot a piece of sponge on both ends.

Sew the elf on the top chalkboard border by hand.

Size (W x H x D):
21 5/8" x 12 5/8" x 3"
[55 cm x 32 cm x 8 cm]

Material

Polar fleece, each approximately 59" [150 cm] wide, and flannel/cotton fabrics, each approximately 43 1/4" [110 cm] wide:

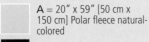 A = 20" x 59" [50 cm x 150 cm] Polar fleece natural-colored

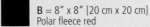 B = 8" x 8" [20 cm x 20 cm] Polar fleece red

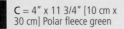 C = 4" x 11 3/4" [10 cm x 30 cm] Polar fleece green

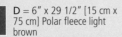 D = 6" x 29 1/2" [15 cm x 75 cm] Polar fleece light brown

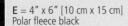 E = 4" x 6" [10 cm x 15 cm] Polar fleece black

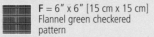 F = 6" x 6" [15 cm x 15 cm] Flannel green checkered pattern

G = 6" x 43 1/4" [15 cm x 110 cm] Natural-black small checkered pattern

H = 2" x 13 3/4" [5 cm x 35 cm] Natural-black large checkered pattern

I = 6" x 6" [15 cm x 15 cm] Natural-red checkered pattern

Additional supplies:

19 3/4" x 15" [50 cm x 38 cm] freezer paper

• Synthetic stuffing (base, snowmen)
• 10 black buttons, dia. 3/16" [5 mm] (eyes)
• 10 black buttons dia. 3/8" [10 mm] (for sewing on the arms)
• 5 carrot-shaped buttons
• 6 decorative buttons
• 1 broom, 6 1/4" [16 cm] long
• 1 wicker wreath, dia. 3" [8 cm]
• Black wool (hair) 6" [15 cm]
• Black pipe cleaner
• Black twist embroidery thread

Let it Snow

This happy snowman family feels their best on the cool window sill and keeps away drafts with the cuddly polar fleece.

Draft Stopper

Preparation

You will find the templates on page 85. Enlarge the templates A - I by 200%, copy onto freezer paper, and cut out accurately.

Cutting

The measurements include 1/4" [0.75 cm] seam allowances. For the templates a 1/4" [0.75 cm] seam allowance must be added all around.

1x

10 3/8" x 25 1/2" [26.5 cm x 65 cm]

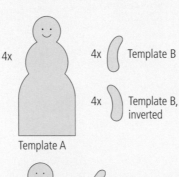

4x Template A

4x Template B

4x Template B, inverted

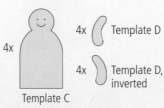

4x Template C

4x Template D

4x Template D, inverted

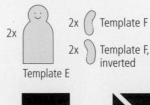

2x Template E

2x Template F

2x Template F, inverted

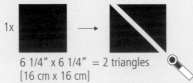

1x

6 1/4" x 6 1/4" = 2 triangles [16 cm x 16 cm]

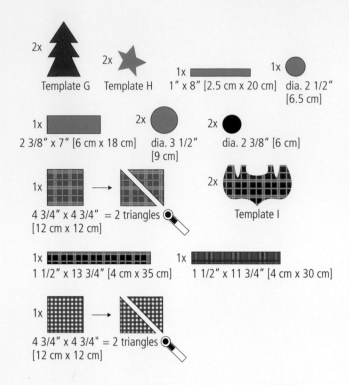

2x Template G   2x Template H   1x 1" x 8" [2.5 cm x 20 cm]   1x dia. 2 1/2" [6.5 cm]

1x 2 3/8" x 7" [6 cm x 18 cm]   2x dia. 3 1/2" [9 cm]   2x dia. 2 3/8" [6 cm]

1x 4 3/4" x 4 3/4" = 2 triangles [12 cm x 12 cm]   2x Template I

1x 1 1/2" x 13 3/4" [4 cm x 35 cm]   1x 1 1/2" x 11 3/4" [4 cm x 30 cm]

1x 4 3/4" x 4 3/4" = 2 triangles [12 cm x 12 cm]

For each scarf only one of both triangles will be needed.

Piecing

Snowmen

For each sew together 2 snowman pieces that are the same size with the right sides together according to the method "stitching and turning with freezer paper" (see basic course on page 12), leave an opening for turning.

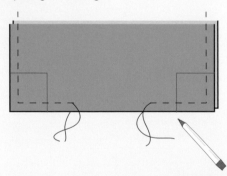

Bottom corners are sewn on the lower corners. For this draw a 1 3/16" [3 cm] square on each bottom corner on the front and back side for the large and medium snowmen. For the small snowman the square is 1/2" [1.5 cm].

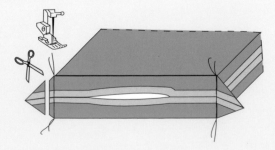

Push down the side seams of the snowman inward onto the bottom to the marking lines. This results in two triangles that stick out on the sides. Sew both corners along the drawn marking lines and trim up to a 3/8" [1 cm] seam allowance.

Turn the piece, fill with stuffing, close the opening by hand.

For the arms sew together 2 inverse pieces with the right sides together, turn, fill, close the opening. Make all of the snowmen and arms in this manner. Stitch down the arms with one button each on the shoulders.

Sew on 2 small buttons for the eyes and a carrot-shaped button for the nose. Embroider the mouth with black quilting thread.

Accessories from left to right

1. Snowman with a red cap (from the left, etc.)

Cap

Fold a triangle made from fabric B ■ 3/8" [1 cm] outward on the long side, sew together the short sides with the right sides together, turn the cap, sew onto the head with several stitches.

Scarf

Sew a triangle made from fabric F ▦ at an interval of 3/8" [1 cm] to the outer edge, fray the border.

Star

Make a star according to template H made from fabric D ■ according to the method "stitching and turning appliqué" (see basic course on page 13), and embellish with a button. Sew the points of the star onto the arms of the snowman.

2. Small snowman

Hair

Pull the wool through on the top of the head with an embroidery needle and knot.

Scarf

Tie around the strip made from fabric D ■ and sew on the decorative button.

Vest

For the vest lay both cuts made from fabric G ▦ on top of each other with the right sides together, sew together foot-wide all around except for an opening for turning, cut the seam allowances in the curves until just before the seam, turn the piece, close the opening, and sew together the shoulder seams (see the markings on the template: S1 on S1, S2 on S2).

3. Snowman with a Christmas Tree

Hair

See the description for the second small snowman.

Scarf

Sew a triangle made from fabric I ▦ at an interval of 3/8″ [1 cm] to the outer edge, fray the border.

Christmas Tree

Make the Christmas tree according to template G made from fabric C ■ like the star (stitching and turning appliqué). Sew on 2 decorative buttons in the center, and sew the Christmas tree onto the snowman's arms.

4. Snowman with Earmuffs

Earmuffs

2x

Line both circles made from fabric E ■ all around with small running stitches and pull each together to form a ball. Lay the pipe cleaner on top of the head, shape both ends into a loop, and cover each with a ball. Sew the earmuffs on by hand.

Scarf

Sew a strip made from fabric G ▦ at an interval of 3/8″ [1 cm] to the outer edge and fray.

Sew on the decorative buttons and broom.

5. Snowman with a Hat

Hat

Close the strip for the hat border made from fabric D ■ into a ring. Lay the circle with the 2 1/2″ [6.5 cm] diameter as a hat top flat onto the ring and inset.

For the brim, sew together both circles with a 3 1/2″ [9 cm] diameter foot-wide all around with the right sides together. In the inside center cut out a 1 3/16″ [3 cm] circle through both layers, turn the piece.

Slide the top part of the hat (consisting of the hat border and top) through the opening of both circles of fabric so that the open side of the ring lies between both layers of brim fabric. Cut the seam allowances in the curve.

Turn the open (inner) fabric edges of the brim inward close to the edge (so that the borders are finished) and sew both borders onto the top part of the hat (ring) by hand.

Scarf

Sew strips made from fabric H ▦ at an interval of 3/8″ [1 cm] to the outer edge and fray.

Sew on the wicker wreath.

Base

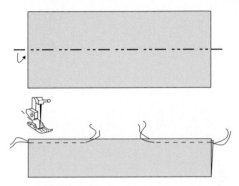

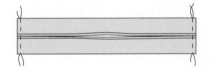

Fold the triangle made from fabric A ☐ lengthwise with the right sides together and sew together to the right and the long edge—except for an approximately 6″ [15 cm] opening for turning in the center area.

Adjust the "tube" in such a way that the stitched seam lies in the center. Sew together both short sides foot-wide.

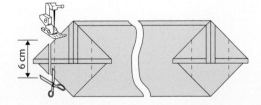

Adjust the "tube" again so that the seam is even with the edge on one side. Fold the ends in such a way that 2 points are formed on each side.

6 cm

Mark a stitching line on all four points of the 2 3/8″ [6 cm] wide spot and quilt. Cut triangles up to a seam allowance of 3/8″ [1 cm]. Turn the tube, fill with stuffing, and close the opening by hand.

Finishing

Stitch down the snowmen onto the tube by hand.

Waiting for Santa Claus

Whoever captures this cuddly blanket will not voluntarily give it up. It is an invitation to a feeling of well-being. The center section is made of double polar fleece and has a different color on each side. For this blanket no backing or interfacing is necessary. Because the trim is sewn together from sections of various widths that are freely chosen, it is completed in no time.

Size:
**53 1/2" x 69 1/4"
[136 cm x 176 cm]**

Material

For the blanket (center section):

Double polar fleece, approximately 59" [150 cm] wide:

 A = 74 3/4" x 59" [190 cm x 150 cm] Double face polar fleece Natural-rust-colored

For the trim:

Cotton fabrics, each approximately 43 1/4" [110 cm] wide:

 B = 17 3/4" x 43 1/4" [45 cm x 110 cm] Natural-colored flower pattern

 C = 10" x 43 1/4" [25 cm x 110 cm] Rust-colored striped pattern

 D = 11 3/4" x 43 1/4" [30 cm x 110 cm] Rust-natural-green checkered pattern

 E = 11 3/4" x 43 1/4" [30 cm x 110 cm] Ochre-natural-green small checkered pattern

 F = 11 3/4" x 43 1/4" [30 cm x 110 cm] Natural-rust-colored small checkered pattern

 G = 11 3/4" x 43 1/4" [30 cm x 110 cm] Rust-colored

Additional supplies:

 8" x 15" [20 cm x 38 cm] freezer paper

- Approximately 6 1/2 yards [6 m] natural-colored rick rack, 3/4" [2 cm] wide
- Matching sewing thread

Feel-good cuddly blanket

Preparation

You will find the templates on page 86. They do not include seam allowances. Enlarge templates A and B by 200%, copy onto freezer paper, and cut out accurately.

Cutting

Measurements include seam allowances of 1/4" [0.75 cm].

1x — 53 1/2" x 69 1/4" [136 cm x 176 cm]

1x — 10" x 10" [25 cm x 25 cm] (Fabrics D, E, F, G)

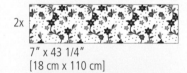

2x — 7" x 43 1/4" [18 cm x 110 cm]

1x — 7" x 43 1/4" [18cm x 110 cm]

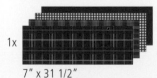

1x — 7" x 31 1/2" [18 cm x 80 cm] (Fabrics D, E, F, G)

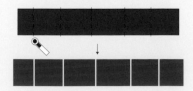

Cut the strips of fabrics **B - G** into sections with different widths between 4 3/4" [12 cm] and 10 1/4" [26 cm].

Piecing

Blanket with a trim

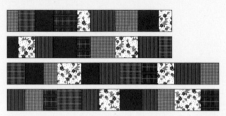

Sew together the sections of fabric to form 2 rows at a length of 55" [140 cm] and 2 rows at a length of 71" [180 cm]. Make sure that on each corner the same fabric patterns to not meet.

For the trim, fold the strips lengthwise with the reverse sides together and press. Tuck both lengthwise edges 1/4" [0.75 cm] inward, and press. Turn in the short ends 3/4" [2 cm] each.

Position all 4 trim sections up to the pressed crease over the polar fleece edge and pin on the natural-colored side—hereafter called the top side. Fold each bottom edge of the trim outward. Quilt the top edges of the trim close to the edge. Quilt the rick rack on the stitched top trim edge all around. Now fold the bottom trim edge around the fleece over the seam of the quilted top trim edge, and sew by hand with small hem stitches. At the corners overlap the trim strips, and close the short outer edges by hand.

Appliqué

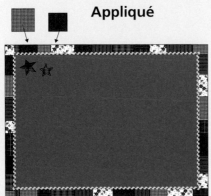

Press the freezer paper template A for the large star onto the right side of fabric **D**. Cut out the piece with a 3/8" [1 cm] seam allowance all around and pin on a corner (measured approximately 10" [25 cm] from both outer borders) on the top side of the blanket. The freezer paper points upward. Fix a square made from fabric **F** on the back side the same size of the star on the front side. Along the freezer paper edge quilt on the star and the square in one step. Remove the freezer paper. Trim the square on the back side with a seam allowance of 3/8" [1 cm] along the seam line so that a star is also visible here.

Position the small star somewhat off-center next to the other star. Press template B on fabric **E**, and for the back side use a 10" [25 cm] square made from fabric **G** and appliqué in the same way in one step.

Size:
17 3/8" x 14 3/16"
[44 cm x 36 cm]
(Star pillow)
12 3/16" x 15"
[31 cm x 38 cm]
(Grain pillow)

Material

Star Pillow

For the stars:

Double polar fleece, approximately 59" [150 cm] wide:

 A = 20" x 39 3/8" [50 cm x 100 cm] Double face polar fleece natural-rust-colored

For the pocket:

Cotton fabrics, each approximately 43 1/4" [110 cm] wide:

 B = 6" x 10" [15 cm x 25 cm] Natural-colored flower pattern

 F = 6" x 6" [15 cm x 15 cm] Natural-rust-colored small checkered pattern

Additional supplies:

• 1 natural-colored button, dia. 3/8" [1 cm]
• Approximately 2 1/4 yards [2 m] natural-colored rick rack, 3/8" [1 cm] wide
• Synthetic stuffing

Grain pillow

Cotton fabric, approximately 43 1/4" [110 cm] wide:

 D = 17 3/4" x 43 1/4" [45 cm x 110 cm] Rust-natural-green checkered pattern

For the filling:

• 35 oz. [1 kg] spelt grain

Star pillow

Preparation

You will find the templates on page 86. Make a template. First enlarge the template by 200%.

Cutting

Measurements include seam allowances of 1/4" [0.75 cm]. For template C add a 3/4" [2 cm] seam allowance all around.

2x   Template C

To cut out template C place the marked edge of the crease on the fold.

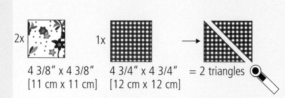

2x   4 3/8" x 4 3/8" [11 cm x 11 cm]   1x   4 3/4" x 4 3/4" [12 cm x 12 cm]   = 2 triangles

Piecing

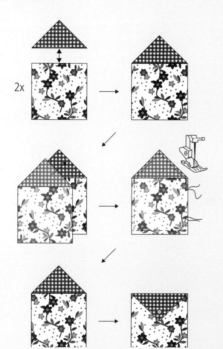

Sew the triangles made from fabric F ⊞ with the long side onto each square made from fabric B ◩. This results in 2 squares with a "roof." Position the pieces with the right sides together and sew together foot-wide all around—except for an opening for turning. Turn the piece, close the opening.

Sew the left, bottom, and right edge of the little pocket in the center of a piece made from fabric A ◣ (rust-colored side of the double polar fleece). Fold the triangle downward and fix with a button.

Pin together both stars made from polar fleece. On the back side the natural-colored side faces outward. Sew together all around with an interval of 3/4" [2 cm] to the outer edge as follows: join the pillow side with the little pocket and back side of the pillow with the right sides together. When sewing together include the rick rack. Pay attention to the opening for filling. Fill the pillow with stuffing. Close the opening. Quilt once again at an interval of 3/8" [1 cm] to the outer edge.

Grain Pillow

You will find the pattern on page 87. Make a template. First enlarge the pattern by 200%. To cut template D place the marked edge of the crease onto the fold and add a 1/4" [0.75 cm] seam allowance all around.

Position the fabric pieces with the right sides together, sew together foot-wide all around—except for an opening for turning—slightly cut the seam allowances in the curves, turn the piece, and work out the seams.

Fill with spelt, close the opening by hand.

Jingle Bells

The classy curtains and the matching table runner create a festive spirit in subtle, natural-gold pattern fabrics. The little bells bring Christmas chimes to mind, the prairie points and the little stitched pockets that are individually decorated add the final touches.

Size:
9 1/2" x 13 3/4"
[24 cm x 35 cm]
(incl. hangers)

Material
for 4 curtains

For the front sides and backing:

Cotton fabrics, each approximately 43 1/4" [110 cm] wide:

 A = 31 1/2" [80 cm] Natural-colored

B = 17 3/4" [45 cm] Gold pattern

C = 10" [25 cm] Natural-gold pattern

D = 6" [15 cm] Natural-colored with gold hearts

E = 6" [15 cm] Natural-colored with gold writing

For the batting:

 11 3/4" x 47 1/4" [30 cm x 120 cm] Volume fleece Freudenberg HH 650

Additional supplies:

- 12 little, gold bells, approximately 3/8" [1 cm] tall
- Matching sewing and quilting thread
- Decorations for the little pockets, according to preference

Curtains

Cutting

Measurements include 1/4" [0.75 cm] seam allowances.

For the front sides, backing, prairie points, and hangers

8x 7" x 7" [17.5 cm x 17.5 cm]

8x 1 3/16" x 43 1/4" [3 cm x 110 cm]

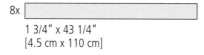

8x 1 3/4" x 43 1/4" [4.5 cm x 110 cm]

16x 3 3/4" x 3 3/4" [9.5 cm x 9.5 cm]

8x 4" x 4" [10 cm x 10 cm]

4x 4 3/4" x 4 3/4" [12 cm x 12 cm]

16x 2 1/2" x 4" [6.5 cm x 10 cm]

For the batting

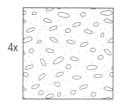

4x 10 3/8" x 10 3/8" [26.5 cm x 26.5 cm]

Piecing

Curtains

The 4 curtains are made inversely.

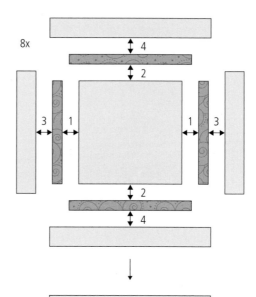

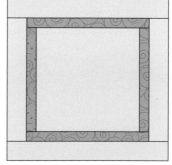

Border the 8 center sections made of fabric **A** ☐ with strips made from fabric **B** ▨; this means that for the first border first sew the strips onto the center square foot-wide on the left and right, press, then sew on the strips at the top and bottom. Sew on the second border with strips made from fabric **A** ☐ in the same way.

Little Pockets

For the 8 little pockets, position 2 squares each made from fabric **C** 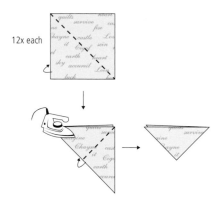 with the right sides together and sew together all around except for an opening for turning. Turn the pieces, close the opening by hand. Quilt the top edges of the little pockets close to the edge.

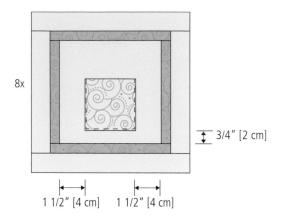

8x

3/4" [2 cm]

1 1/2" [4 cm]   1 1/2" [4 cm]

Pin the pockets onto the curtain piece (3/4" [2 cm] from the bottom gold border, 1 1/2" [4 cm] from both sides) and sew on at the left, bottom, and right close to the edge.

Prairie Points

12x each

Fold the squares for the prairie points made from fabrics **D** and **E** diagonally with the reverse sides together and press. Fold the resulting triangles diagonally once again and press.

Hangers

For the hangers, position 2 pieces each with the right sides together and sew together foot-wide onto the long side, turn the hangers, quilt both lengthwise edges close to the edge.

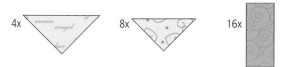

4x   8x   16x

You will need a total of 4 large prairie points for the center of the curtain, 8 small prairie points for the sides, as well as 16 hangers.

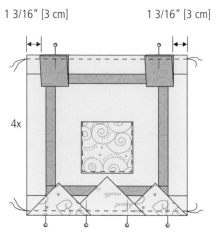

1 3/16" [3 cm]   1 3/16" [3 cm]

4x

Double fold the hangers lengthwise. Pin 2 hangers each on the top border of a curtain piece pointing inward. The distance to both outer edges is 1 3/16" [3 cm].

Fix the prairie points pointing inward on the bottom border of the curtain piece with the right sides together. Arrange the pieces from fabrics **D** 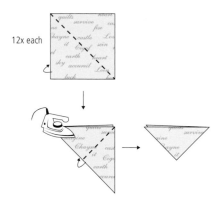 on the outside and the pieces from fabric **E** 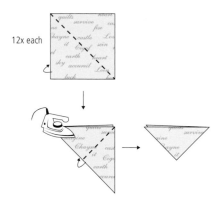 in the center.

Secure the hangers and prairie points with auxiliary stitching (3/16" [0.5 cm] from the outer edge).

Prepare a total of 4 pieces in this way.

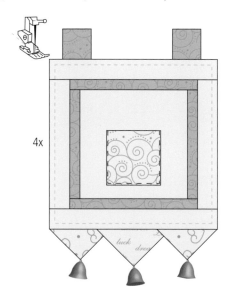

4x

Finishing

Pin a curtain piece that is prepared with the hangers and prairie points on a bordered piece with a pocket and a correspondingly big piece of volume fleece with the right sides together. Sew together all around except for an opening for turning. Turn the piece, and work out the corners and seams. Close the opening by hand.

Quilt at an interval of 3/8" [1 cm] to the outer edge. Sew the small bells onto each tip of the prairie points by hand. Decorate the little pockets according to preference.

Festive table runner

Cutting

Measurements include 1/4" [0.75 cm] seam allowances.

For the center section

6x

1 3/16" x 18 3/4"
[3 cm x 47.5 cm]

2x

10 13/16" x 18 3/4"
[27.5 cm x 47.5 cm]

2x

1 3/4" x 18 3/4"
[4.5 cm x 47.5 cm]

1x

11" x 18 3/4"
[28 cm x 47.5 cm]

3x

1 3/8" x 43 1/4"
[3.5 cm x 110 cm]

For the Prairie Points

4x

4" x 4"
[10 cm x 10 cm]

6x

4 3/4" x 4 3/4"
[12 cm x 12 cm]

For the backing

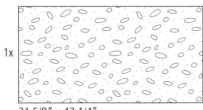

1x

21 5/8" x 43 1/4"
[55 cm x 110 cm]

For the batting

1x

21 5/8" x 43 1/4"
[55 cm x 110 cm]

Piecing

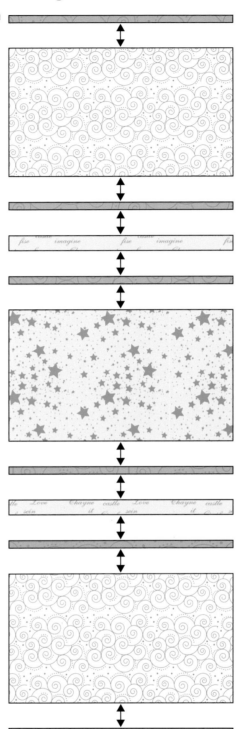

For the center section lay out the cuts from fabrics **B** ▣, **C** ▣, **E** ▨ and **F** ▣ according to the schematic drawing and sew together foot-wide.

Size:
19 3/4" x 43"
[50 cm x 109 cm]

Material

For the front side:

Cotton fabrics, each approximately 43 1/4" [110 cm] wide:

 **A** = 6" x 43 1/4" [15 cm x 110 cm] Natural-colored

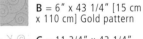 **B** = 6" x 43 1/4" [15 cm x 110 cm] Gold pattern

 **C** = 11 3/4" x 43 1/4" [30 cm x 110 cm] Natural-gold pattern

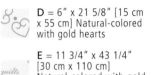 **D** = 6" x 21 5/8" [15 cm x 55 cm] Natural-colored with gold hearts

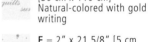 **E** = 11 3/4" x 43 1/4" [30 cm x 110 cm] Natural-colored with gold writing

 **F** = 2" x 21 5/8" [5 cm x 55 cm] Natural-colored with gold stars

For the backing:

21 5/8" x 43 1/4" [55 cm x 110 cm] Volume fleece Freudenberg HH 650

For the batting:

55 x 110 cm Volumenv-lies Freudenberg HH 650

Additional supplies:

• 10 small, gold bells, approximately 3/8" [1 cm] tall
• Matching sewing and quilting thread

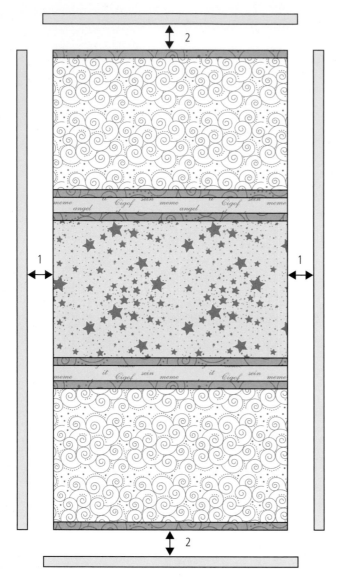

Finishing

With the right sides together, pin the finished top on the backing fabric and interfacing, sew together all around except for an opening for turning. Trim the interfacing and backing to the size of the front side, turn the piece, work out the corners and seams, and close the opening by hand.

Border the piece with strips made from fabric **A** ☐ ; first sew the strips on the long sides, separate the third strip, and sew on the short sides.

Prepare the prairie points as described with the curtains.

Like with the curtains, pin the triangles, pointing inward, on the short sides of the table runner with the right sides together, alternate fabrics **D** ◨ and **E** ▨ . Fabric **E** ▨ is arranged on each outer side. Secure the pieces with an auxiliary seam.

Quilt the outer border and between all strips in the ditch with matching quilting thread. Mark both center diagonals on the center rectangle, and starting from here, mark parallel lines 2" [5 cm] to both sides and quilt. Carefully press the piece with steam.

Sew the little bells on each tip of the prairie points by hand.

Size:
14" x 17"
[35.5 cm x 45.5 cm]

Material
For 2 placemats

For the front sides and binding:
Cotton fabrics, each approximately 43 1/4" [110 cm] wide:

 A = 11 3/4" [30 cm]
Natural-colored

 B = 4" [10 cm]
Brown

 C = 8" [20 cm]
Natural-green checkered pattern

 D = 8" [20 cm]
Natural-green pattern

 E = 6" [15 cm]
Light green marbled pattern

 F = 11 3/4" [30 cm]
Dark green marbled pattern

For the backing:
 D = 15 3/4" x 43 1/4"
[40 cm x 110 cm]

For the batting:
 15 3/4" x 45" [40 cm x 115 cm] Thermolam

 6" x 15 3/4" [15 cm x 40 cm] Volume fleece Freudenberg HH 650

Additional supplies:
6" x 15" [15 cm x 38 cm] Freezer paper

• Matching sewing and quilting thread

In the Fir Forest

These cute placemats with an edging made from two different fabrics and an appliquéd little fir tree suit breakfast or coffee tables decorated for Christmas. You can put bread, cookies, or nuts in the basket, which consists only of a base and little trees standing upright.

Placemats

Preparation

You will find the templates on page 87. Copy template A including markings onto freezer paper and cut out accurately.

Cutting

Measurements include 1/4" [0.75 cm] seam allowances. For the appliqué piece according to template A, 1/4" [0.75 cm] seam allowances are needed.

For the center sections

2x

9" x 13"
[23 cm x 33 cm]

For the border strips

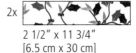

3x

1" x 43 1/4"
[2.5 cm x 110 cm]

2x
2 1/2" x 10"
[6.5 cm x 25 cm]

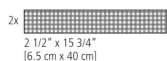
2x
2 1/2" x 11 3/4"
[6.5 cm x 30 cm]

2x
2 1/2" x 15 3/4"
[6.5 cm x 40 cm]

2x
2 1/2" x 17 3/4"
[6.5 cm x 45 cm]

For the appliqués

4x
Template A

2x
Template A

For the backing

2x

15 3/4" x 20" [40 x 50 cm]

For the batting

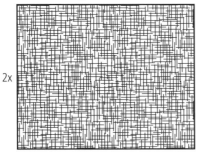

2x

15 3/4" x 20" [40 cm x 50 cm]

For the binding

4x

2 1/2" x 43 1/4" [6.5 cm x 110 cm]

Piecing

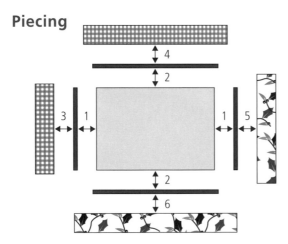

Border the rectangles made from fabric **A** ☐ with strips made from fabric **B** ■, first sewing the strips on the left and right, then on the top and bottom. Press the seam allowances behind the dark fabric. The second border made from fabric **C** ⊞ is sewn around in the order: left / top / right / bottom.

Quilting

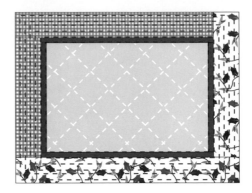

Pin the finished top on the Thermolam and backing fabric. On the light center section draw diagonal markings at an interval of 2" [5 cm] with the help of a 45° line cutting ruler and quilt with 1/8" [3 mm] stitch length. Quilt the stitched strips in the ditch. Mark the checkered border at an interval of 3/8" [1 cm] lengthwise and quilt.

Making the Fir Trees

Make two fir trees according to the method "stitching and turning appliqué with freezer paper" (see basic course on page 13), in addition, use volume fleece HH 650. Trim the seam allowances, cut the seam allowances in the valleys. According to template A make a cut in a fabric layer, turn the fir trees through this opening. Work out the seams and tips, press the pieces. With matching thread, quilt the tree cores similarly to the template or according to your own preference.

Finishing

After quilting, trim the backing and batting to the size of the front side. Place the trees on the prepared placemats in such a way that they slightly protrude beyond the second edging on the right and bottom, quilt all around close to the edge.

Apply the continuous binding by sewing together the 4 strips made from fabric **F** ■ onto the short sides. Proceed as is described in the basic course under "continuous binding" on page 14.

Basket

Preparation

You will find the templates on pages 88-89. Copy templates B and C, including markings onto freezer paper and cut out accurately. For the base, make a template out of paper or cardboard from template D.

Cutting

Measurements include 1/4″ [0.75 cm] seam allowances. For the patterns 1/4″ [0.75 cm] wide seam allowances are needed.

For the inside and outside base

2x

11 3/4″ x 15 3/4″
[30 cm x 40 cm]

For the batting

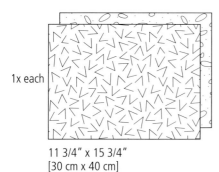

1x each

11 3/4″ x 15 3/4″
[30 cm x 40 cm]

For the fir trees

2x each

Template B (= results in 1 fir tree each)

4x each

Template B (= results in 2 fir trees each)

4x each

Template C (= results in 2 fir trees each)

2x each

Template C (= results in 1 fir tree each)

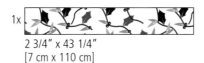

8x   6x

Template B (= Batting for 8 fir trees)   Template C (= Batting for 6 fir trees)

For the binding

1x

2 3/4″ x 43 1/4″
[7 cm x 110 cm]

Piecing

Base

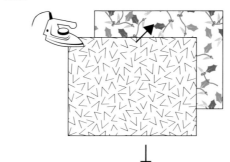

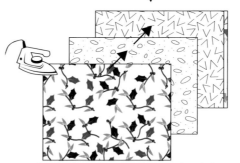

To make the base lay the glossy side of the S 520 interfacing onto the wrong fabric side of a rectangle made from fabric A 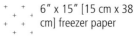 and press.

Size:
10 5/8" x 14 1/2"
[27 cm x 37 cm]
Height:
6" [15 cm]

Material

For the base and the trees:

Cotton fabrics, each approximately 43 1/4″ [110 cm] wide:

 A = 15 3/4″ [40 cm] Natural-green pattern

 B = 8″ [20 cm] Green with white dots

 C = 8″ [20 cm] Green pattern

 D = 8″ [20 cm] Light green marbled pattern

 E = 8″ [20 cm] Dark green marbled pattern

 F = 8″ [20 cm] Green with dots

For the batting:

 11 3/4″ x 15 3/4″ [30 cm x 40 cm] Interfacing Freudenberg S 520

 11 3/4″ x 15 3/4″ [30 cm x 40 cm] Volume fleece Freudenberg HH 650

 15 3/4″ x 45″ [40 cm x 115 cm] Thermolam

Additional supplies:

6″ x 15″ [15 cm x 38 cm] freezer paper

• Matching sewing and quilting thread

Tip: To avoid puckering, do not move the iron. Firmly press the iron on top of each spot for a few seconds until the fabric and the fusible interfacing are smoothly joined.

Then place the double-sided adhesive HH 650 on top of the matt side of the S 520, and the second rectangle made from fabric A with the right fabric side pointing up. Press with steam until all 4 layers are joined.

With matching thread, quilt a diagonal grid (line spacing at 2" [5 cm]), as is described with the placemats.

Copy the outline of the base from template D on Fabric **A** with the help of the template and cut.

Fir Trees

Make the fir trees according to the method "stitching and turning with freezer paper" (see basic course on page 12). However, work with an opening for turning on the lower border and use Thermolam as batting.

A total of 8 small fir trees according to template C and 6 large fir trees according to template D are required.

Turn the trees, the opening for turning remains open. Quilt all around close to the edge; quilt the tree cores.

Pin the evenly distributed trees with the open edges outward all around the base (the tops of the trees point toward the center of the base and lie flat) and secure with auxiliary stitching.

Finishing

Bind the base, as is described in the basic course on page 14 under "continuous binding." The only difference is that no corners are sewn here.
Set up the trees. Fix the tips of the trees that touch or overlap with small stitches by hand.

Size (W x H x D):
17 3/8" x 14 3/16" x 8"
[44 cm x 36 cm x 20 cm]

Material

For the outer sides and lining:

Cotton fabrics, approximately 55" [140 cm] wide:

 A = 11 3/4" x 55" [30 cm x 140 cm] Light pink with white dots

 B = 23 5/8" x 55" [60 cm x 140 cm] Pink-white striped pattern

 C = 20" x 55" [50 cm x 140 cm] Brown with pink dots

 D = 10" x 55" [25 cm x 140 cm] Brown-pink pattern

 E = 10" x 55" [25 cm x 140 cm] Pink with brown dots

 F = 8" x 15 3/4" [20 cm x 40 cm] Light blue-pink pattern

 G = 31 1/2" x 55" [80 cm x 140 cm] Pink with white dots

For the batting:

 39 3/8" x 59" [100 cm x 150 cm] Volume fleece Freudenberg HH 650

 59" x 21 5/8" [150 cm x 55 cm] Fast2Fuse

Additional supplies:

• 5 1/2 yards [5 m] pink alcantara band, 1/8" [3 mm] wide
• 5 1/2 yards [5 m] natural-colored alcantara band, 1/8" [3 mm] wide
• 1 yard [1 m] brown rick rack
• 1 yard [1 m] red-white checkered ruched ribbon
• 2 x 24 different motif buttons (2 each of one motif)
• 2 round buttons
• Brown fabric pen

Advent House

This house has it all! Behind each roller blind there is a motif in the form of a stitched motif button. One side of the roof can be opened, and for each motif button you can find a fitting—naturally filled—little sack in the house.

A special advent calendar

Preparation

You can find the template for the gable on page 88. It already includes 1/4" [0.75 cm] seam allowances.

Cutting

Measurements include 1/4" [0.75 cm] seam allowances.

For the back side of the house

8x
3" x 3"
[7.5 cm x 7.5 cm]

8x
3" x 5 5/16"
[7.5 cm x 13.5 cm]

10x
1 3/4" x 3" [4.5 cm x 7.5 cm]

1x
2" x 16" [5 cm x 40.5 cm]

1x
1 3/4" x 16" [4.5 cm x 40.5 cm]

1x
3" x 16" [7.5 cm x 40.5 cm]

For the front side of the house

6x
3" x 3"
[7.5 cm x 7.5 cm]

6x
5 5/16" x 6 1/2"
[13.5 cm x 16.5 cm]

6x
3" x 5 5/16"
[7.5 cm x 13.5 cm]

9x
1 3/4" x 3"
[4.5 cm x 7.5 cm]

1x
2" x 16" [5 cm x 40.5 cm]

1x
1 3/4" x 16" [4.5 cm x 40.5 cm]

2x
3" x 5 5/16"
[7.5 cm x 13.5 cm]

2x
5 5/16" x 6 1/2"
[13.5 cm x 16.5 cm]

For both gable sides

8x
3" x 3"
[7.5 cm x 7.5 cm]

8x
3" x 5 5/16"
[7.5 cm x 13.5 cm]

12x
1 3/4" x 3" [4.5 cm x 7.5 cm]

2x
6 1/4" x 9" [16 cm x 22.5 cm]

2x
1 3/4" x 9" [4.5 cm x 22.5 cm]

2x
3" x 9" [7.5 cm x 22.5 cm]

For the lining

2x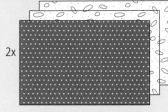
10 1/4" x 16" [26 cm x 40.5 cm]

2x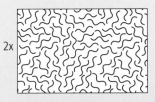
9 5/8" x 15 3/8" [24.5 cm x 39 cm]

2x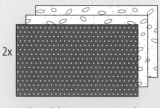
15" x 9" [38 cm x 22.5 cm]

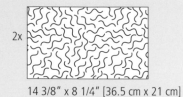

2x

14 3/8" x 8 1/4" [36.5 cm x 21 cm]

For the base

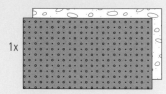

1x

9" x 16"
[22.5 cm x 40.5 cm]

1x

9" x 16" [22.5 cm x 40.5 cm]

1x

8 1/4" x 15 3/8"[21 cm x 39 cm]

1x

2 3/4" x 49 5/8" [7 cm x 126 cm]

For the roof

1x

2 3/4" x 18 1/2" [7 cm x 47 cm]

2x

8" x 18"
[20 cm x 46 cm]

2x

8" x 18"
[20 cm x 46 cm]

2x

7 1/4" x 17 1/2"
[18.5 cm x 44.5 cm]

For the little sacks

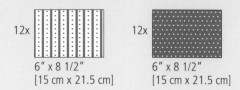

12x 6" x 8 1/2"
[15 cm x 21.5 cm]

12x 6" x 8 1/2"
[15 cm x 21.5 cm]

Piecing

Roller blinds

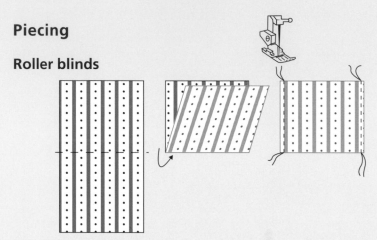

Fold the rectangles for the roller blinds lengthwise with the right sides together and sew together both sides foot-wide. The top edge remains open; turn the roller blinds here.

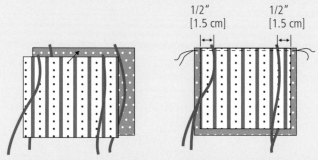

1/2"
[1.5 cm]

1/2"
[1.5 cm]

Fix the open edges of the stitched and turned roller blinds each with auxiliary stitching close to the edge on the window background squares made from fabric **A** . Here include four 2" [5 cm] sections of the pink alcantara band per roller blind. Arrange two bands each on the top side of the roller blind and two bands at the bottom. The distance to the outer edge of the roller blind is 1/2" [1.5 cm] each.

Stitch a total of 22 windows including the roller blind.

The back side of the house

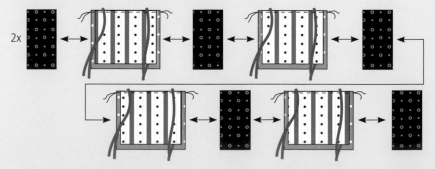

2x

Lay out and alternate 5 rectangles made from fabric **C** and 4 window pieces with roller blinds into a row, and sew together the pieces. From here make 2 rows.

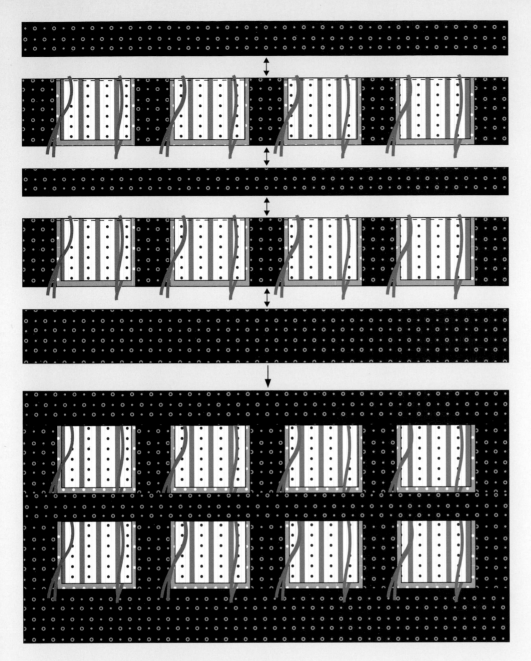

Sew the 3 strips correspondingly above, at the center of, and below the rows of windows as is described under "cutting / the back side of the house."

The front side of the house

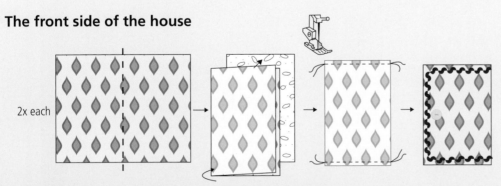

2x each

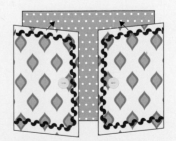

On the front side of the house first sew on the doors. For this fold the rectangles with the right sides together, place HH 650 underneath, and sew together both short edges. One long side remains open. Turn the doors; quilt rick rack on both sides. Sew a round button on each door (see illustration).

Place the doors onto the background fabric made from fabric A ▦ and secure with auxiliary stitching.

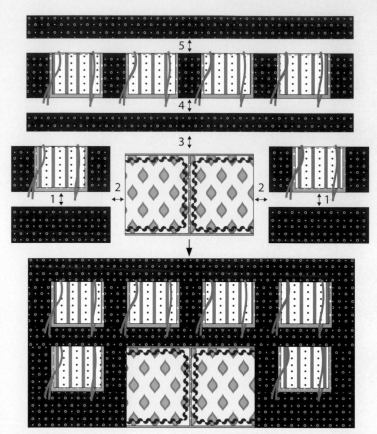

Sew the front side of the house in the same manner as the back side, taking the corresponding pieces of the cutting list. Include the doors while sewing together the rows.

Gable sides

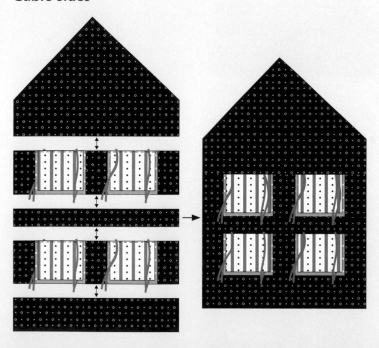

Sew both gable sides in the same way as the back of the house, taking the corresponding pieces of the cutting list. Angle the rectangle for the gable according to the template that is true to the original.

Joining the house pieces and lining

Pin HH 650 on each outer piece and lining piece. Put together the outer house pieces and the lining pieces each into a ring.

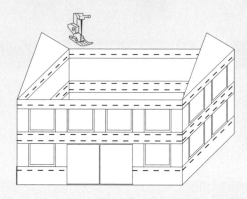

Quilt the strips above and below the windows at an interval of 3/8" [1 cm] all around on the ring of the outer side of the house.

Position both "rings" into each other with the right sides together and sew together on the top border. Turn the piece, put Fast2Fuse between the layers of interfacing. Press the pieces with steam until all layers are joined.

Base

For the base stack the layers as follows: Fabric C ▨, HH 650, Fast-2Fuse, HH 650, fabric D ▨. The right fabric sides always point outward. Press the pieces with steam until all layers are joined. Insert the base at the bottom house border and sew on with the binding strips made from fabric G ▨ fold down the trim, and sew by hand.

Roof

For the roof, stack the layers as follows: fabric E ▨, fabric D ▨, HH 650. The two fabrics are right sides together. On three sides sew together, leaving the top edge of the roof open. A total of two roof parts are produced in this way. Connect parts.

Insert the rectangle made from Fast2Fuse. Press the pieces with steam until all layers are joined. Sew together the open roof edges close to the edge and bind with the strip made from fabric A ▨.

Sew on a ruched ribbon close to the edge on the bottom roof edge. Sew only one roof side on the top house border by hand; the other remains open.

Little sacks

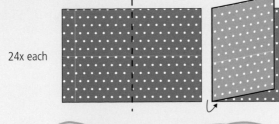

24x each

For the little sacks fold up the rectangles to 6" x 4 1/4" [15 cm x 10.75 cm] with the right sides together. For each little sac prepare a piece of natural-colored alcantara band that is 8" [20 cm] long, double it, and put between the layers of fabric in the top third of the long side.

Sew together a short and long side of the little sack, including the band. Turn the little sacks and fold 3/4" x 3/16" [2 cm x 0.5 cm] inward on the top border and hem.

Finishing

Sew a different motif button on each little sack. Sew the matching piece of each button on the 22 windows and on one of the two sides of the door.

With a fabric pen write the numbers 1 to 24 on the outer sides of the roller blinds and door pieces.

Stylish

This placemat pair is a classy, cool beauty. Not only does the silverware fit into the integrated cutlery pocket, but also the self-made napkin with classic mitered corners.

Classy placemats with silverware pockets

Preparation

You will find the templates on page 83. For template ❶ the seam allowance is marked. The appliqué pieces ❷ to ❺ do not include seam allowances because they are not needed.

Note: The appliqué templates ❹ to ❺ are drawn inversely.

For the appliqués, first copy the individual motif pieces from the original size template onto vliesofix. The numbers indicate the sequence in which the pieces will be appliquéd. Place the vliesofix onto the template in such a way that the uncoated side points upward. Copy the outlines of the motif pieces. Cut out the pieces freehand and press onto the wrong fabric side of the corresponding fabrics. Then cut out accurately.

Cutting

Measurements include 1/4" [0.75 cm] seam allowances.

For the cutlery pockets

4x
4" x 6 3/4" [10 cm x 17 cm]

2x
2 1/2" x 5" [6.5 cm x 13 cm]

4x
4" x 6 3/4" [10 cm x 17 cm]

For the backing

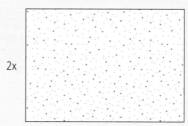
2x
15" x 19" [38 cm x 48 cm]

For the center sections

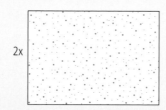
2x
9 5/8" x 13 5/8"
[24.5 cm x 34.5 cm]

For the batting

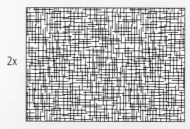
2x
15" x 19" [38 cm x 48 cm]

For the border strips

3x
1" x 43 1/4" [2.5 cm x 110 cm]

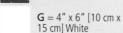
3x
2 1/2" x 43 1/4" [6.5 cm x 110 cm]

For the binding

4x
2 1/2" x 43 1/4" [6.5 cm x 110 cm]

Size:
13 3/4" x 17 3/4"
[35 cm x 45 cm]

Material
for 2 placemats

For the front side and binding:

Cotton fabrics, each approximately 43 1/4" [110 cm] wide:

A = 11 3/4" [30 cm]
White with little silver dots

B = 8" [20 cm]
Dark blue

C = 10" [25 cm]
Light blue with stars

D = 11 3/4" [30 cm]
Blue striped pattern

E = 6" [15 cm]
Light blue with silver dots

F = 4" x 10" [10 cm x 25 cm]
Medium blue

G = 4" x 6" [10 cm x 15 cm] White

For the backing:

A = 15 3/4" x 43 1/4" [40 cm x 110 cm]

For the batting:

15 3/4" x 45 1/4" [40 cm x 115 cm] Thermolam

4" x 15 3/4" [10 cm x 40 cm] Volume fleece Freudenberg 281

Additional supplies:

2" x 17 3/4" [5 cm x 45 cm] vliesofix (fusible)

2" x 17 3/4" [5 cm x 45 cm] embroidery interfacing

• 2 silver heart-shaped buttons

Piecing

Front Side

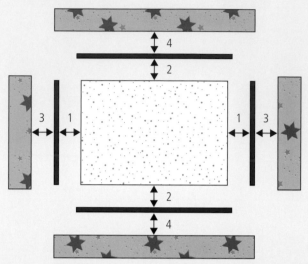

Border the center section made from fabric **A** ☐ with strips made from fabric **B** ■; this means first sew on the strips foot-wide on the left and right, press, then sew foot-wide on the top and bottom. Sew on the strips made from fabric **C** ▨ in the same sequence.

Cutlery pocket

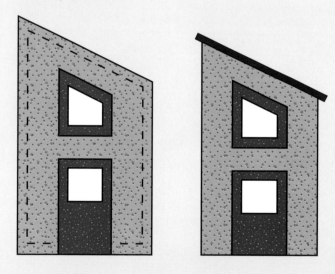

For the cutlery pocket angle two rectangles made from fabric **E** on the top border according to template ❶.

Pull off the backing paper of the appliqué motifs and press the motifs onto the background fabric (pay attention to the sequence!). The right side of the fabric faces upward.

Place the appliqué motifs with embroidery interfacing on the backing of the house piece ❶ (this prevents the fabric from puckering) and appliqué the pieces with matching thread and a compact zigzag stitch (see basic course "machine appliqué with satin stitch" on page 13). Remove the embroidery interfacing.

Place the finished appliquéd house piece on a rectangle made from fabric **E** ▨ with the right sides together and a correspondingly large piece of volume fleece. Sew together foot-wide on both sides and on the bottom border. Trim the excess fabric and interfacing to the width of the seam allowance. Turn the piece.

Fold the strip for the roof (fabric **B** ■) lengthwise with the reverse sides together and sew on at the top border like a binding. Leave 3/8" [1 cm] excess on each side.

Quilting

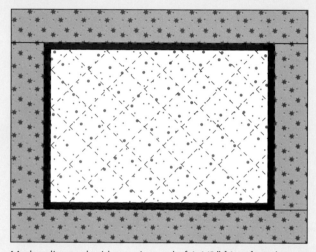

Mark a diagonal grid at an interval of 1 1/2" [4 cm] on the center section. Baste the piece with pins on the Thermolam and backing fabric. With matching thread quilt the grid and the stitched strips in the ditch.

Finishing

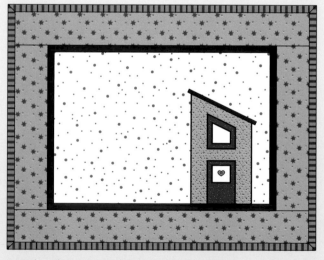

Sew the silverware pocket by hand onto the placemat. Sew the heart-shaped button onto the door.

Trim the interfacing and backing to the size of the front side. Apply the continuous binding (see basic course on "continuous binding" on page 14).

Enchanting silver-white napkins

Cutting

Measurements include 1/4" [0.75 cm] seam allowances

2x

15 3/4" x 15 3/4" [40 cm x 40 cm]

Stitching

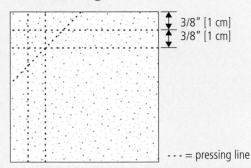

3/8" [1 cm]
3/8" [1 cm]

- - - = pressing line

Press all 4 edges two times 3/8" [1 cm] to the reverse side of the fabric. Then mark a diagonal over the inner intersection of the pressed lines and also press to the left. Fold back the corner again.

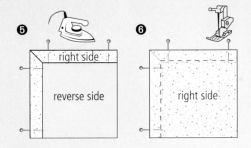

❺ right side / reverse side
❻ right side

Fold the outer edges all around on the outer pressing line on the reverse side of the fabric again and no longer fold back (step 1).

Lay the fabric of a corner on top of each other with the right sides together. The creases of the diagonals are directly on top of each other. Pin, and sew the diagonals. Secure the beginning and end of the seam (step 2).

Cut excess fabric to a 3/16" [0.5 cm] wide seam allowance, and pull open the folded fabric again (step 3).

The hem is now folded twice on the front side, and the seam allowances of the stitched corners are visible. Press the seam allowances apart and turn the hem on the back side (step 4).

Turn the piece so that the back side is on top, work out the corner, pin, if necessary, and press the hem flat (step 5).

Repeat steps 2 to 5 for the other three corners.

Lastly, quilt the entire inner edge of the trim close to the edge (step 6).

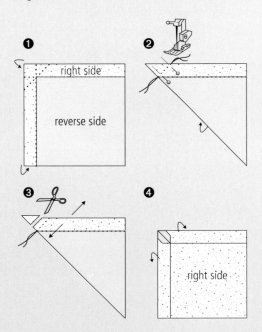

❶ right side / reverse side
❷
❸
❹ right side

Size:
14 3/16" x 14 3/16"
[36cm x 36 cm]

Material
for 2 napkins

Cotton fabric, approximately
43 1/4" [110 cm] wide:

A = 17 3/4" [45 cm]
White with small stars

Christmas Star

The tablecloth in classic country style colors brings a homely spirit to the room. The top piece with the squares and the border strips is sewn together quickly. The rick rack is adorned by stars that are made according to the method of the stitching and turning appliqué. The star-shaped stand up display completes the tablecloth perfectly.

Size:
48" x 48"
[122cm x 122 cm]

Material

For the front side and the binding:

Cotton fabrics, each approximately 43 1/4" and 59" [110 cm and 150 cm] wide:

 A = 6" [15 cm]
Natural-colored pattern

 B = 6" [15 cm]
Yellow striped pattern

 C = 6" [15 cm]
Yellow diagonal checkered pattern

 D = 6" [15 cm]
Yellow with little stars

 E = 6" [15 cm]
Yellow pattern

 F = 6" [15 cm]
Red marbled pattern

 G = 6" [15 cm]
Red with white dots

 H = 6" [15 cm]
Red pattern

 I = 6" [15 cm]
Red pattern

 K = 6" [15 cm]
Green striped pattern

 L = 6" [15 cm]
Green pattern

 M = 6" [15 cm]
Green marbled pattern

 N = 6" [15 cm]
Dark green pattern

Materials continued on page 66

Festive country style tablecloth

Cutting

Measurements include 1/4" [0.75 cm] seam allowances.

For the center section

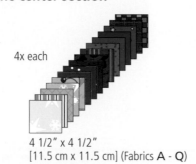

4x each

4 1/2" x 4 1/2"
[11.5 cm x 11.5 cm] (Fabrics **A - Q**)

For the first border

4x

6 1/2" x 32" [16.5 cm x 81.5 cm]

4x

6 1/2" x 6 1/2"
[16.5 cm x 16.5 cm]

For the second border

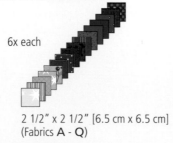

6x each

2 1/2" x 2 1/2" [6.5 cm x 6.5 cm]
(Fabrics **A - Q**)

For the backing

1x

51 3/16" x 51 3/16" [130 cm x 130 cm]

For the batting

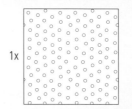

1x

51 3/16" x 51 3/16" [130 cm x 130 cm]

For the edging

5x

2 1/2" x 43 1/4" [6.5 cm x 110 cm]

3x each
Template A

3x each
Template A, inverted

3x each
Template B

3x each
Template B, inverted

Preparation

You will find the templates for the stars (A - B) on page 91. First enlarge the templates by 200%. Copy each of the 4 stars onto freezer paper according to templates A and B and cut out accurately.

Continuation of the materials

 O = 6" [15 cm]
Green with small yellow stars

 P = 6" [15 cm]
Red-green pattern

 Q = 6" [15 cm]
Red-green-yellow small checkered pattern

 R = 43 1/4" [110 cm]
Black pattern

For the star appliqués:

 S = 4" [10 cm]
Yellow dotted pattern

 T = 4" [10 cm]
Yellow marbled pattern

 U = 4" [10 cm]
Ochre dotted pattern

 V = 4" [10 cm]
Ochre striped pattern

For the backing:

 A = 51 3/16" x 59"
[130 cm x 150 cm]

For the batting:

 51 3/16" x 59"
[130 cm x 150 cm]
Volume fleece
Freudenberg 249

Additional supplies:

 4" x 6" [10 cm x 15 cm]
freezer paper

• Approximately 5 yards [4.5 m] natural-colored rick rack
• 1 bag of Rinske's Dijon buttons
• Matching sewing and quilting thread

Piecing

Center section

Lay out the large squares made from fabrics **A - Q** as is shown in the illustration and first sew together foot-wide into rows. Alternately press the seam allowances of the rows to the left and right. Then piece together the 8 rows.

Sew strips made from fabric **R** ■ onto the center section to the left and right. Extend both remaining strips of fabric **R** ■ first left and right with a square made of the same material. Then sew these strips onto the center tablecloth piece at the top and bottom.

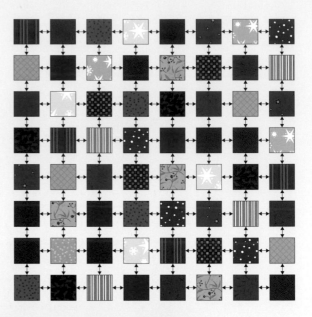

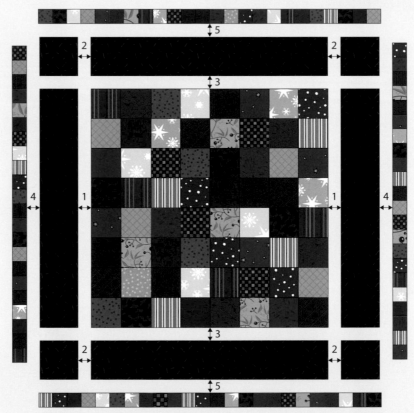

Lay out the small squares as is shown in the illustration and sew together to form 4 rows. Sew on the completed strips.

Joining the layers

See the basic course on page 10.

Quilting

Mark each second center diagonal of the large blocks and quilt. Quilt the stitched strips in the ditch. Quilt the squares of the outer border in a zigzag pattern.

Star appliqués

Make 3 large stars from fabrics **S**, **T**, **U**, and **V** according to template A, and 3 small stars according to template B using the method "stitching and turning appliqué with freezer paper" (see basic course on page 12).

Finishing

Pin rick rack in curved lines onto the border made from fabric **R** ■ and sew.

Arrange the stars on the rick rack and sew on with a button.

Trim the volume fleece and backing fabric to the size of the front side.

Apply the continuous binding, for this, sew together the 5 strips made from fabric **R** ■ onto the short sides. Proceed as is described in the basic course under "continuous binding" on page 14.

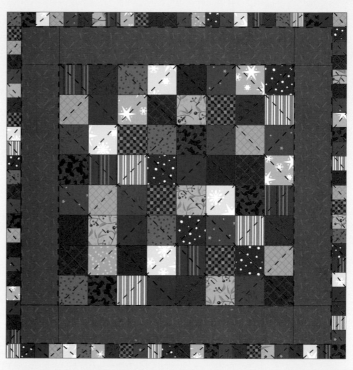

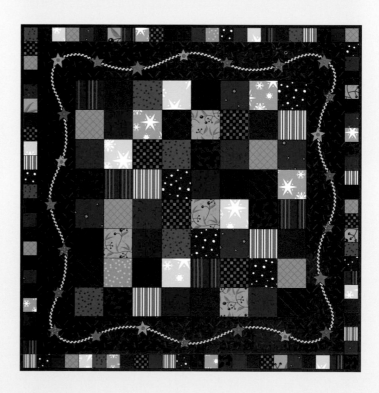

Sizes of the stars
(without the wooden rod):
Approximately 7"
[18 cm] dia. (larger star)
Approximately 5 1/2"
[14 cm] dia. (smaller star)

Material

For each 1 large star plant poke:

Cotton fabrics, each approximately 43 1/4" [110 cm] wide:

 C = 10" x 21 5/8"
[25 cm x 55 cm]
Yellow diagonal checkered pattern

 V = 4" x 8" [10 cm x 20 cm] Ochre striped pattern

Additional supplies:

 10" x 15" [25 cm x 38 cm] freezer paper

• Synthetic stuffing
• 1 round natural-colored button, dia. 1/2" [1.5 cm]
• 1 wooden rod dia. 3/8" [1 cm], 13 3/4" [35 cm] long

For each 1 small star plant poke:

Cotton fabrics, each approximately 43 1/4" [110 cm] wide:

 T = 6" x 11 3/4"
[15 cm x 30 cm]
Yellow marbled pattern

 U = 4" x 8" [10 cm x 20 cm] Ochre dotted pattern

Additional supplies:

 10" x 10" [25 cm x 25 cm] freezer paper

• Synthetic stuffing
• 1 natural-colored heart-shaped button, dia. 1/2" [1.5 cm]
• 1 wooden rod dia. 3/8" [1 cm], 10" [25 cm] long

Decorative star plant pokes

Preparation

You will find the templates on page 91: enlarge by 200%. Copy templates C, D, and E onto freezer paper, and draw the markings for the opening for turning and the rod. Cut out the motif accurately.

Cutting

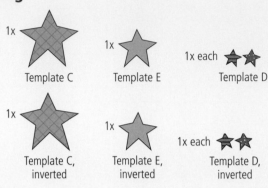

1x   Template C   1x   Template E   1x each   Template D

1x   Template C, inverted   1x   Template E, inverted   1x each   Template D, inverted

Piecing

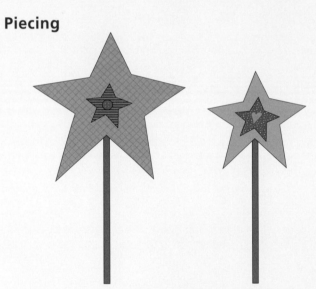

For the large plant poke make a star according to template C from fabric C ▨ and, for the small plant poke a star according to template E from fabric T ▨ using the method "stitching and turning with freezer paper" (see basic course on page 12). Pay attention to the opening for turning and the rod.

Turn the stars and gently fill with stuffing. Close the opening by hand.

Make both attached stars according to templates D from fabric V ▥ (for the large plant poke) and fabric U ▨ (for the small plant poke) in the same way but without stuffing; close the opening. Affix the star with the round button on the large star.

Finishing

Insert the wooden rods into the corresponding opening. Secure somewhat if necessary or sew the opening more narrowly.

Village

Size:
9 1/2" x 27 1/2"
[24 cm x 70 cm]

Material

For two inverse rows of houses:

A = 4" x 11 3/4"
[10 cm x 30 cm]
Natural-colored
marbled pattern

B = 4" x 17 3/4"
[10 cm x 45 cm]
Natural-colored with
little dots

C = 4" x 13 3/4"
[10 cm x 35 cm]
Natural-colored striped
pattern

D = 6" x 10"
[15 cm x 25 cm]
Yellow marbled pattern

E = 4" x 10"
[10 cm x 25 cm]
Yellow with dots

F = 6" x 17 3/4"
[15 cm x 45 cm]
Yellow striped pattern

G = 6" x 15 3/4"
[15 cm x 40 cm]
Red checkered pattern

H = 6" x 8"
[15 cm x 20 cm]
Red marbled pattern

I = 4" x 11 3/4"
[10 cm x 30 cm]
Red with small white
dots

K = 6" x 11 3/4"
[15 cm x 30 cm]
Red with large white
dots

L = 4" x 17 3/4"
[10 cm x 45 cm]
Green with large white
dots

M = 6" x 15 3/4"
[15 cm x 40 cm]
Green with little dots

N = 4" x 8"
[10 cm x 20 cm]
Green striped pattern

Continuation of materials
on page 72

This exceptional table or window decoration with an accordion fold form is sewn from two inverse rows of houses that is used from both sides. With the Thermolam Plus, it stands on its own. The decorative key ring is also pieced together from two inverse sides.

Stand up accordion fold houses

Preparation

You will find the templates on pages 89 - 92. They do not include seam allowances.

For each door and window of the front and back side make a template from freezer paper. Press the templates with the glossy side onto the back of the corresponding fabrics. The letters on the templates indicate the distribution of the fabric. Cut out fabric pieces with 1/4" [0.75 cm] seam allowances all around. Fold back the seam allowances around the template and baste.

Cutting

Take the measurements for the house and roof pieces of the original size template and add a 1/4" [0.75 cm] seam allowance on each side and cut out the corresponding fabrics (see letters on the templates).

Continuation of the materials

 O = 4" x 15 3/4"
[10 cm x 40 cm]
Black with little stars

 P = 4" x 10"
[10 cm x 25 cm]
Black with little dots

 Q = 4" x 13 3/4"
[10 cm x 35 cm]
Black striped pattern

 R = 4" x 6"
[10 cm x 15 cm]
Black pattern

For the batting:

 11 3/4" x 31 1/2"
[30 cm x 80 cm]
Volume fleece
Freudenberg HH 650

 23 5/8" [60 cm]
Thermolam plus (fusible)

Additional supplies:

 11 3/4" x 15" [30 cm x
38 cm] freezer paper

• Matching sewing thread
• Natural-colored and yellow twist embroidery thread
• Motif buttons according to preference

Piecing

House 1   House 2

House 3   House 4

Sew together the house and roof pieces foot-wide. Sew the extensions on the houses to the right and left.

With matching thread sew the door and window appliqué motifs by hand with fine stitches onto the respective house pieces. Make a small cut into the background fabric on the back of each appliqué motif, remove the basting threads, and remove the freezer paper template with the help of tweezers if necessary. Border the windows with natural-colored twist embroidery thread (2-ply) with stem stitching. Embroider the lattice windows with yellow twist embroidery thread (2-ply) also with stem stitching.

For each individual house cut 2 pieces of Thermolam plus, not adding a seam allowance here.

Lay out both rows of houses according to the schematic drawing and sew together the side seams foot-wide. Make sure that you only sew until the bottom roof edges, and secure the end of the seams.

Lay out the corresponding Thermolam plus pieces on the reverse side of the fabric of each row of houses and press. Place the prepared accordion fold pieces on a HH 650 strip with the right sides together.

Finishing

Position the rows of houses with the right sides together and sew together all around, leaving a piece of the seam open on the bottom border for turning. Trim the excess HH 650, cut the seam allowances in the valleys. Turn the piece. Close the opening by hand. Quilt between the houses in the ditch. Carefully press the rows of houses from both sides with steam until all layers are firmly joined.

The windows and doors of the single houses can be additionally decorated with motif buttons (see photo).

Size:
3 1/2" x 5"
[9 cm x 13 cm]
(without the strap)

Material

For the little pocket, heart, and strap:

Cotton fabrics, each approximately 43 1/4" [110 cm] wide:

 B = 4" x 6" [10 cm x 15 cm] Natural-color dotted pattern

 D = 2" x 10" [5 cm x 25 cm] Yellow marbled pattern

 F = 6" x 11 3/4" [15 cm x 30 cm] Yellow striped pattern

 I = 4" x 6" [10 cm x 15 cm] Red with small white dots

 O = 4" x 10" [10 cm x 25 cm] Black with little stars

 R = 4" x 6" [10 cm x 15 cm] Black pattern

For the lining:

 E = 6" x 11 3/4" [15 x 30 cm] Yellow dotted pattern

For the batting:

 6" x 10" [15 cm x 25 cm] Volume fleece Freudenberg HH 650

 6" x 10" [15 cm x 25 cm] Thermolam plus (fusible)

Additional supplies:

 4" x 15" [10 cm x 38 cm] Freezer paper

- 1 key ring with a snap hook
- Matching sewing thread
- Natural-colored and yellow twist embroidery thread
- Synthetic stuffing

Small key case with a heart

Preparation

You will find the templates on page 93. Prepare the house and roof pieces as is described with "accordion fold."

Cutting

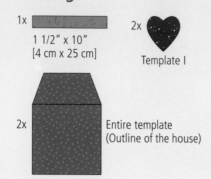

1x — 1 1/2" x 10" [4 cm x 25 cm]

2x — Template I

2x — Entire template (Outline of the house)

Piecing

House and roof

Sew together the house and roof pieces foot-wide.

With matching thread sew the door and window appliqué motifs by hand with fine stitches onto the respective house pieces, and remove the freezer paper, as is described with "accordion fold." Embroider the edging of the window and lattice windows in the same way as with "accordion fold."

For each house piece cut a corresponding piece of Thermolam plus, do not add a seam allowance, and press on the reverse sides of the house pieces. Position both house pieces with the right sides together and sew together on the marked lines. The lower edge, as well as the outlet for the key strap (see marking on the template), remain open.

Lining

For the lining cut 2 pieces according to the entire template made from fabric **E**. Sew together the lining pieces like the front piece, however, leaving an opening for turning in the side seam.

Place the outer key case piece and the lining piece into each other with the right sides together, and sew together foot-wide on the bottom border. Turn the piece through the opening in the lining piece, and close the opening by hand.

Key strap

Fold the strips for the key strap lengthwise with the reverse sides together and press, turn the outer lengthwise edges once again up to the center and press. The strap is now fourfold and 3/8" [1 cm] wide. Fold the short side 3/8" [1 cm] on one end (later the bottom part of the key strap). Quilt the strips close to the edge on the lengthwise sides and bottom.

Heart

Make the heart from fabric **I** according to the method "stitching and turning with freezer paper" (see basic course on page 12). However, before quilting insert the key strap inside on the tip of the heart and include when stitching. Leave the opening for turning open. Turn the heart, fill with stuffing, and close the opening by hand.

Finishing

Insert the key strap through the opening on the roof edge and pull out at the bottom border, insert the key ring with a snap hook, fold down the strap 3/4" [2 cm], and quilt.

**Size (height):
Approximately
27 1/2" [70 cm]**
(incl. cap)

Material

For the body, clothing, and heart:

Polar fleece, each approximately 59" [150 cm] wide, and cotton fabrics, each approximately 43 1/4" [110 cm] and 59" [150 cm] wide:

 A = 20" x 59" [50 cm x 150 cm] Polar fleece red

 B = 10" x 10" [25 cm x 25 cm] Polar fleece natural-colored

C = 20" x 59" [50 cm x 150 cm] Natural-colored

 D = 13 3/4" x 43 1/4" [35 cm x 110 cm] Yellow checkered pattern

 E = 4" x 21 5/8" [10 cm x 55 cm] Yellow-green striped pattern

 F = 8" x 21 5/8" [20 cm x 55 cm] Floral pattern

Additional supplies:

8" x 8" [20 cm x 20 cm] freezer paper

• 2 black buttons, dia. 3/8" [1 cm] (eyes)
• 1 star-shaped natural-colored button, dia. 1" [2.5 cm] (cap)
• 5 natural-colored buttons, dia. 1" [2.5 cm] (cloak)
• Synthetic stuffing
• Granule filling

Santa in Love

Last but not least, St. Nicholas with a heart will put you in the Christmas spirit. Filled with granules, he stands up decoratively. His impressive size also fills a larger entrance area well. The fresh green hearts stand out especially nicely.

A St. Nicholas to fall in love with

Preparation

You will find the templates on page 93: enlarge by 200%. Prepare the cuts for the body according to template A, the arms according to template B, and the cap according to template C. For the heart, copy the outlines, including markings from template D onto freezer paper and accurately cut out.

Cutting

Measurements include 3/8" [1 cm] seam allowances. For the cuts made according to the templates, 3/8" [1 cm] seam allowances each must be added all around.

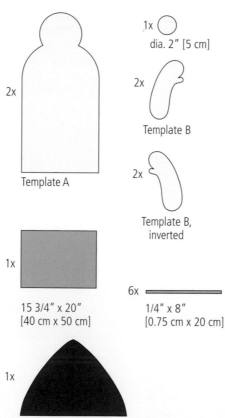

Template A — 2x

1x — dia. 2" [5 cm]

Template B — 2x

Template B, inverted — 2x

15 3/4" x 20" [40 cm x 50 cm] — 1x

6x — 1/4" x 8" [0.75 cm x 20 cm]

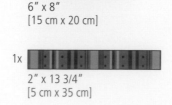 1x — 6" x 8" [15 cm x 20 cm]

1x — 2" x 13 3/4" [5 cm x 35 cm]

 2x

According to the schematic drawing of the cloak (see below)

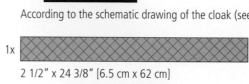 1x — 2 1/2" x 24 3/8" [6.5 cm x 62 cm]

 2x — 5" x 11" [13 cm x 28 cm]

 2x — 4" x 11 3/4" [10 cm x 30 cm]

 2x — Template D

Piecing

Body

Sew together 2 pieces according to template A with 3/8" [1 cm] seam allowance with the right sides together, paying attention to the opening for turning.

On each lower corner sew a bottom corner (as is described with the "draft stopper" on page 36). Here work with a 2" [5 cm] square. Cut seam allowances in the curves. Turn the body. Then fill the top two-thirds of the body with stuffing and the remaining third with granules.

Arms

Sew together 2 pieces each, according to template B with the right sides together, turn, fill with stuffing, and sew on the side of the upper body by hand.

Nose

Gather the circle for the nose, fill with some stuffing, and sew together. Sew on the nose.

Eyes

Sew on both buttons for the eyes.

Beard and moustache

For the beard double the rectangle to 6" x 4" [15 cm x 10 cm], cut both layers of fabric until 3/4" [2 cm] before the edge of the crease at an interval of 3/8" [1 cm]. Sew the beard on the jaw by hand.

For the moustache, tightly join together the 6 strips in the center with thread and sew on directly under the nose.

Cap

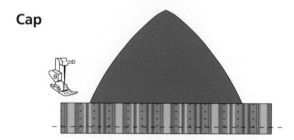

Place the strip for the brim of the cap with the right side on the reverse side of the cap along the bottom border of the piece according to template C and sew with a 3/8" [1 cm] seam allowance.

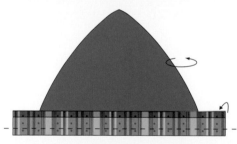

Turn the opposite edge of the trim 3/8" [1 cm] inward, and fold down the strips to the front side.

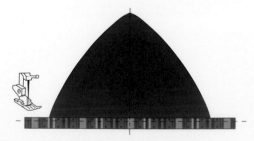

Quilt both edges of the trim close to the edge.

Fold the cap piece halfway with the right sides together and sew together on the long side with a 3/8" [1 cm] seam allowance. Turn the cap.

Fold the tip slightly forward and sew on the decorative button.

Put on the cap and pull sideways until over the base of the beard, sew all around on the head by hand.

Cloak

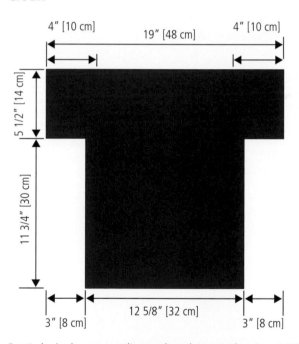

Cut 2 cloak pieces according to the schematic drawing. A 3/8" [1 cm] seam allowance is already included here.

Position the front and back pieces with the right sides together, close both side seams and sleeve seams. Close the shoulder seams (4" [10 cm]).

78

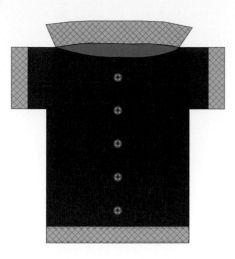

Close the strip for the hem to form a ring and sew as is described with the cap trim.

Close the 2 strips for the sleeve trim to form a ring. Sew each strip on the bottom edge of the sleeve with the right sides together. Fold the trim halfway inward, press 3/8" [1 cm] hem, sew the inner edge of the trim by hand.

Position the pieces for the collar with the right sides together and sew together on both short sides and a long side, turn the collar. Fold the open edges 3/8" [1 cm] inward, sew on the collar by hand on the back neckline of the cloak.

Sew 5 natural-colored buttons evenly on the front side of the cloak.

Heart

Make the heart according to the method "stitching and turning with freezer paper" (see basic course on page 12). Gently fill with stuffing. Close the opening by hand.

Finishing

Pull the cloak over the body. Sew the heart on the right and left side between the hands by hand.

Heart ornaments
Preparation

You will find the templates on page 93. Enlarge template D by 200%, copy onto freezer paper including markings and cut out accurately.

Cutting

2x each

Template D

Stitching

From each fabric make a heart according to the method "stitching and turning with freezer paper" (see basic course on page 12). Gently fill the hearts with stuffing, then close the opening by hand.

Finishing

Separate the satin ribbon into 3 equal sections, double it, and knot both ends. Sew on the knot as a hanger in the center of the heart at the top.

Size (W x H):
5 1/2" x 5"
[14 cm x 13 cm]

Material

For 3 hearts:
Cotton fabrics, each approximately 43 1/4" [110 cm] wide:

 F = 8" x 21 5/8" [20 cm x 55 cm] Yellow-red-green floral pattern

 G = 8" x 21 5/8" [20 cm x 55 cm] Green striped pattern

 H = 8" x 21 5/8" [20 cm x 55 cm] Red with green stars

Additional supplies:
8" x 8" [20 cm x 20 cm] freezer paper

• Synthetic stuffing
• 1 yard [1 m] red satin ribbon, 3/32" [2 mm] wide

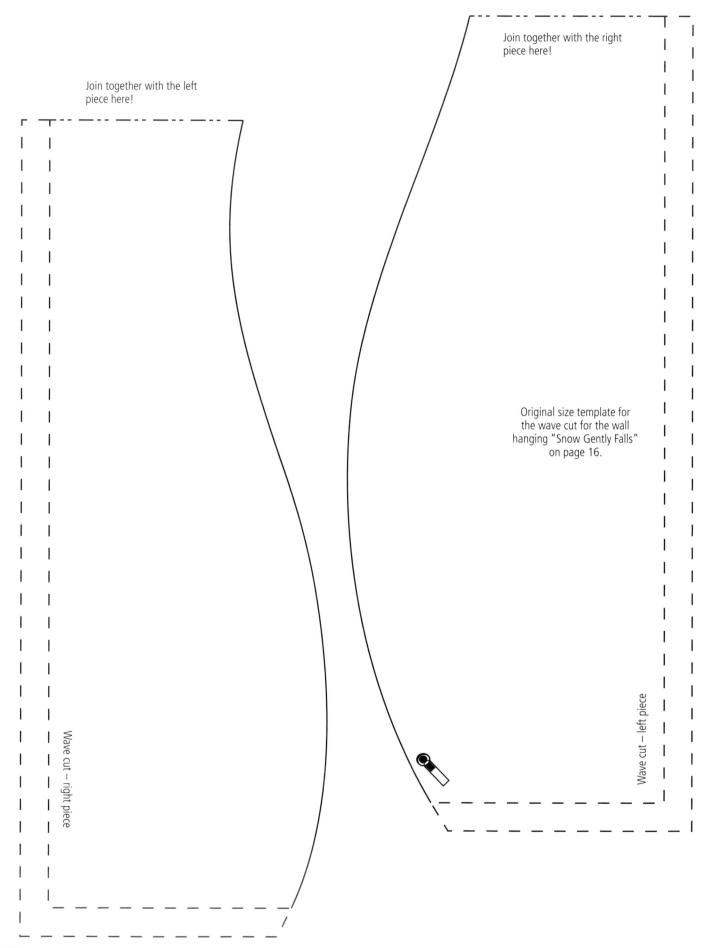

Join together with the left
piece here!

Join together with the right
piece here!

Original size template for
the wave cut for the wall
hanging "Snow Gently Falls"
on page 16.

Wave cut – right piece

Wave cut – left piece

Original size templates (without seam allowances) for the wall hanging "Snow Gently Falls" on page 16. The letters indicate which fabrics to use.

Original size templates (without seam allowances)
for the wall hanging and the Christmas tree stands
"Snow Gently Falls" on page 20.

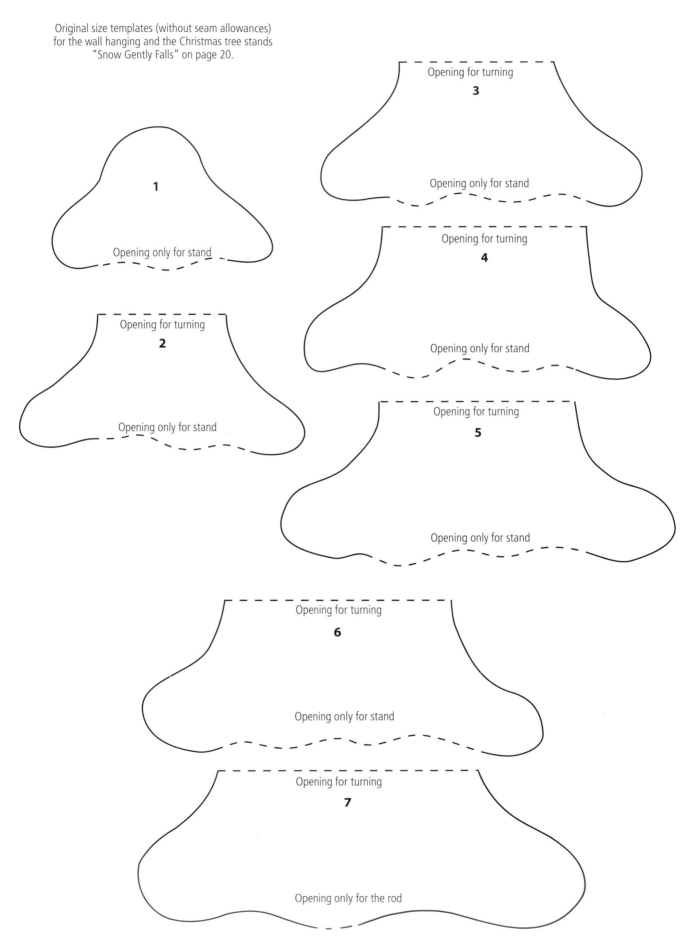

1

Opening only for stand

Opening for turning
3

Opening only for stand

Opening for turning
2

Opening only for stand

Opening for turning
4

Opening only for stand

Opening for turning
5

Opening only for stand

Opening for turning
6

Opening only for stand

Opening for turning
7

Opening only for the rod

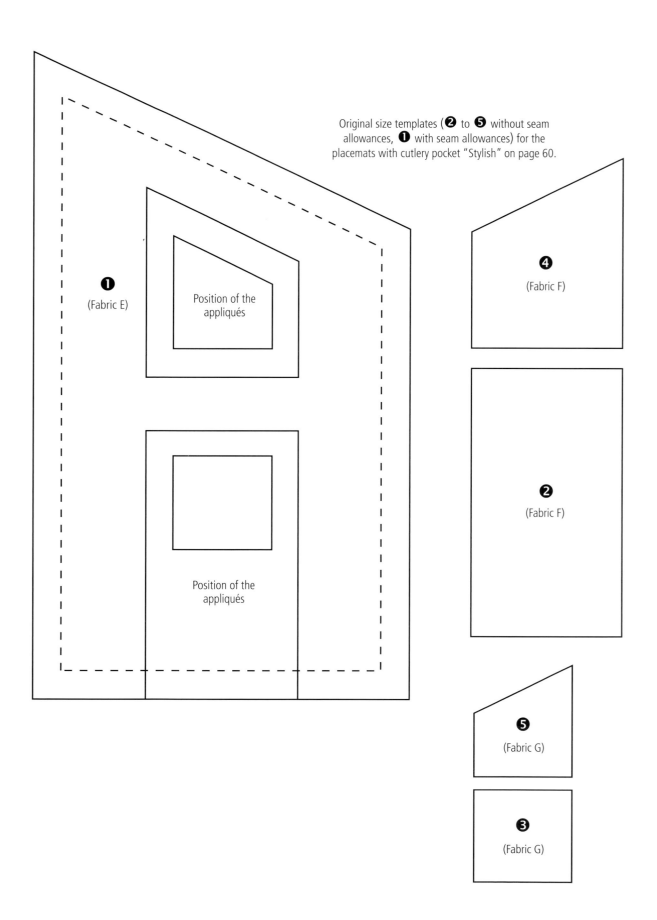

Original size templates (❷ to ❺ without seam allowances, ❶ with seam allowances) for the placemats with cutlery pocket "Stylish" on page 60.

❶
(Fabric E)

Position of the appliqués

Position of the appliqués

❹
(Fabric F)

❷
(Fabric F)

❺
(Fabric G)

❸
(Fabric G)

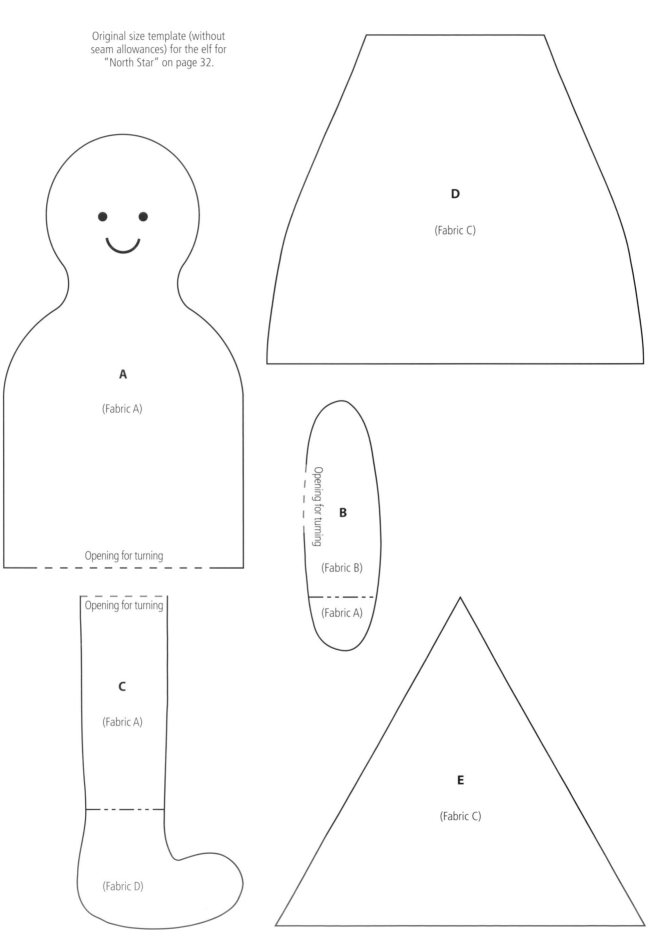

Original size template (without seam allowances) for the elf for "North Star" on page 32.

D

(Fabric C)

A

(Fabric A)

Opening for turning

Opening for turning

B

(Fabric B)

(Fabric A)

Opening for turning

C

(Fabric A)

(Fabric D)

E

(Fabric C)

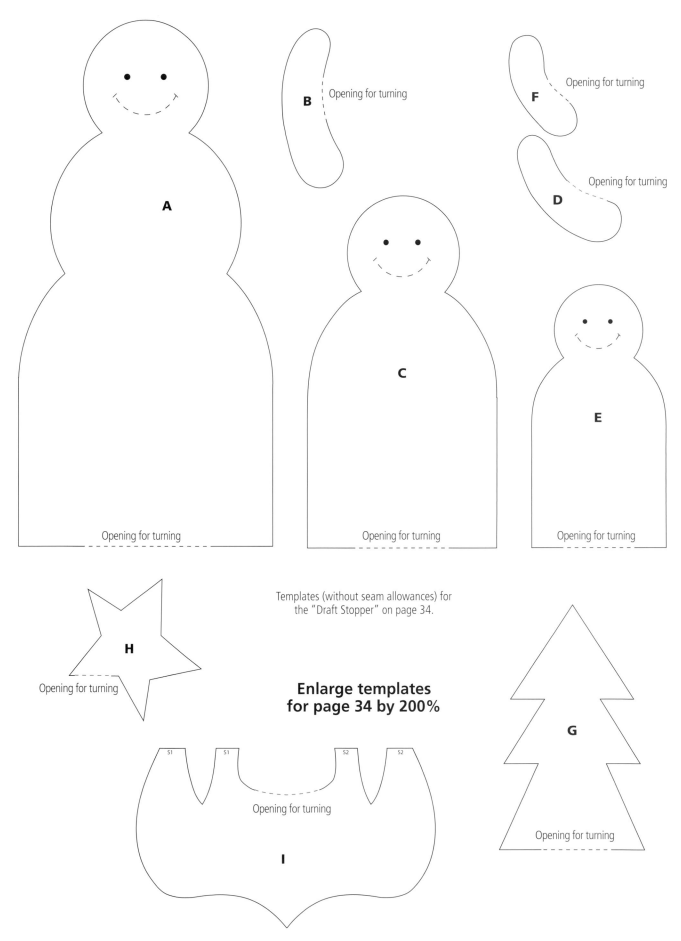

A

B Opening for turning

F Opening for turning

D Opening for turning

C

E

Opening for turning

Opening for turning

Opening for turning

H

Opening for turning

Templates (without seam allowances) for
the "Draft Stopper" on page 34.

**Enlarge templates
for page 34 by 200%**

S1   S1   S2   S2

Opening for turning

I

G

Opening for turning

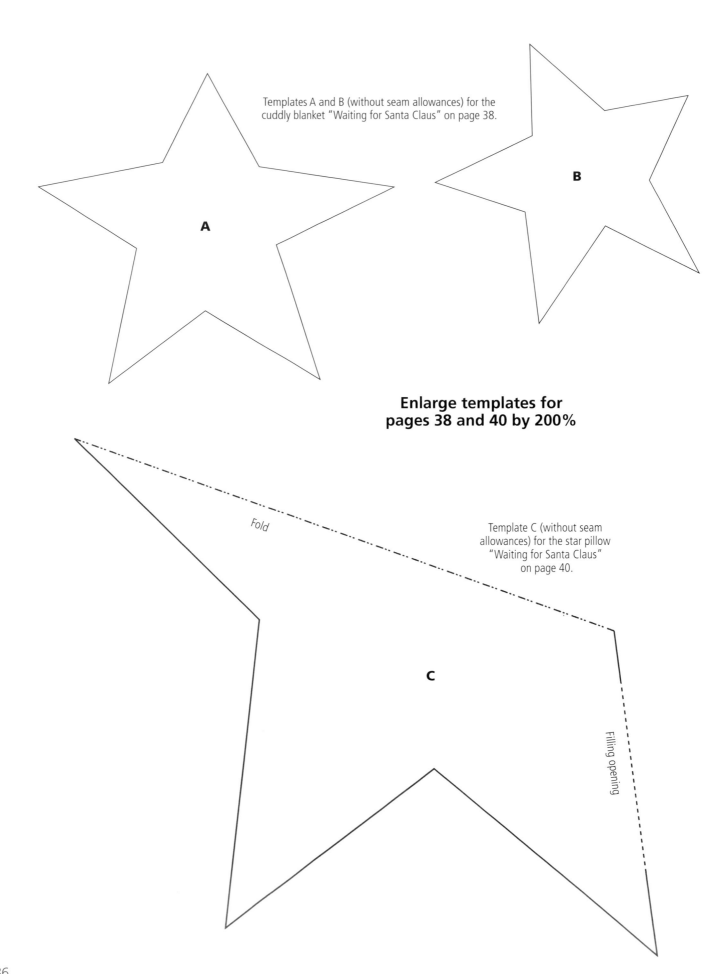

Templates A and B (without seam allowances) for the cuddly blanket "Waiting for Santa Claus" on page 38.

Enlarge templates for pages 38 and 40 by 200%

A

B

Fold

Template C (without seam allowances) for the star pillow "Waiting for Santa Claus" on page 40.

C

Filling opening

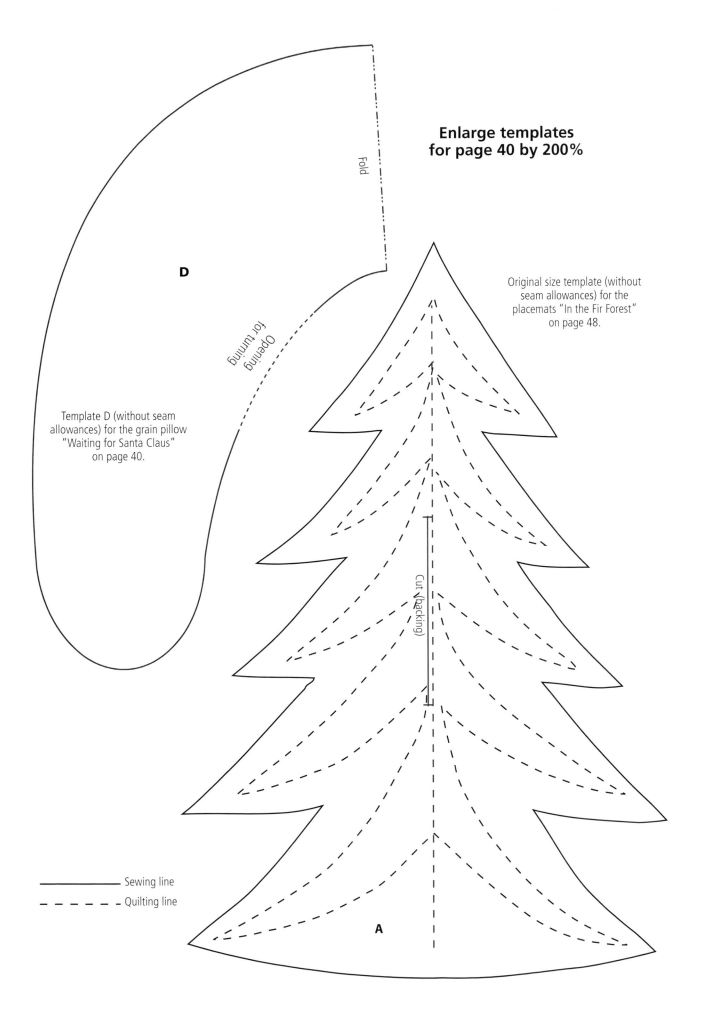

Enlarge templates for page 40 by 200%

Fold

D

Opening for turning

Template D (without seam allowances) for the grain pillow "Waiting for Santa Claus" on page 40.

Original size template (without seam allowances) for the placemats "In the Fir Forest" on page 48.

Cut (backing)

A

—————— Sewing line

- - - - - Quilting line

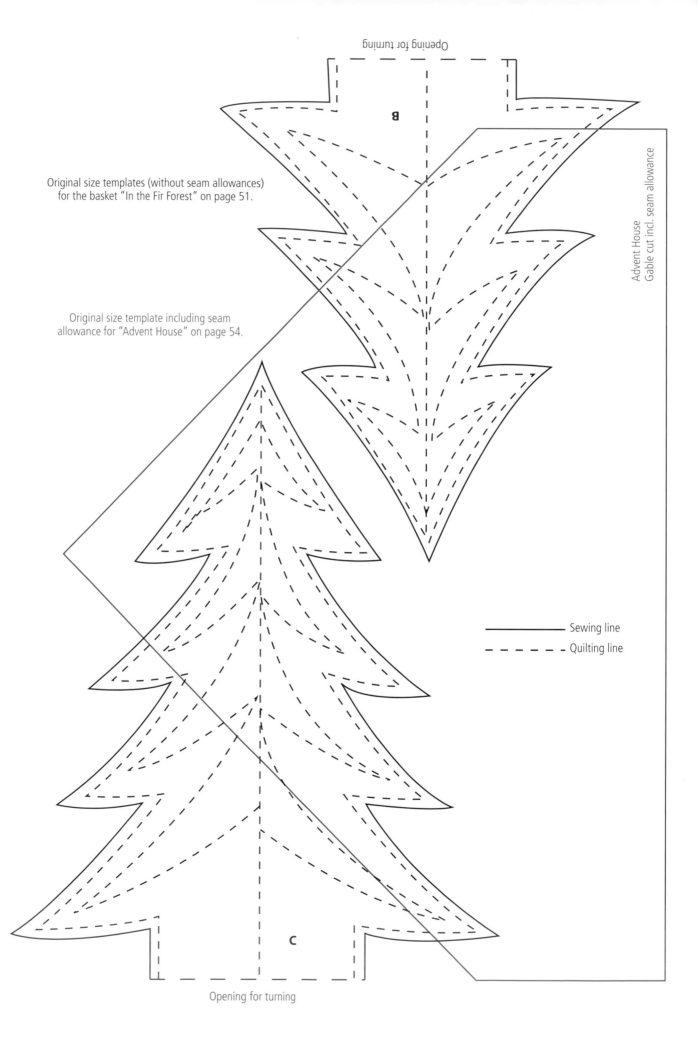

B

Original size templates (without seam allowances) for the basket "In the Fir Forest" on page 51.

Advent House
Gable cut incl. seam allowance

Original size template including seam allowance for "Advent House" on page 54.

——————— Sewing line

– – – – – Quilting line

C

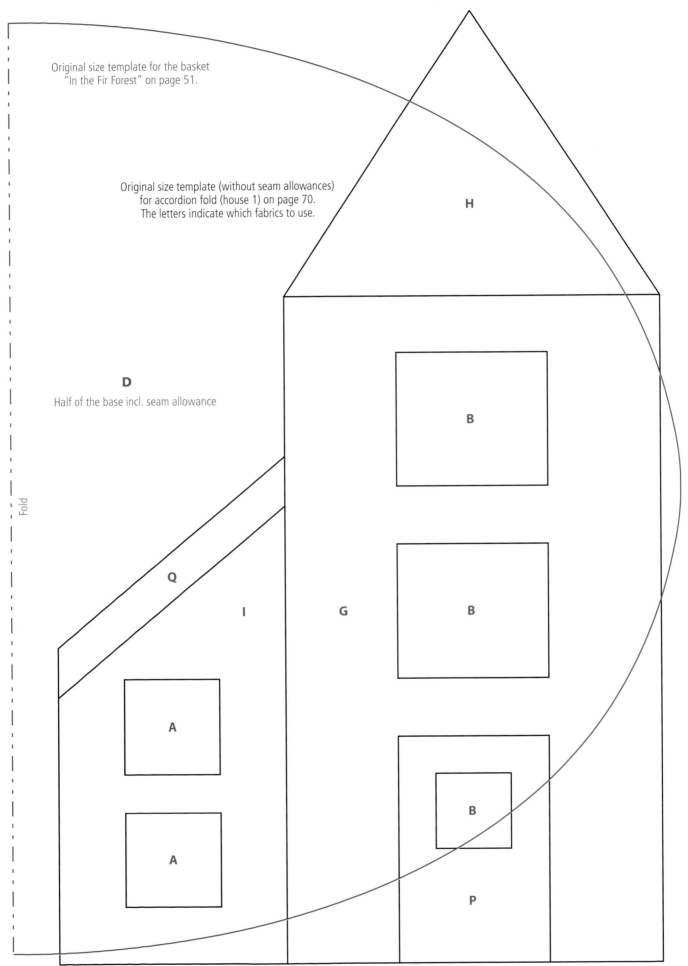

Original size template for the basket
"In the Fir Forest" on page 51.

Original size template (without seam allowances)
for accordion fold (house 1) on page 70.
The letters indicate which fabrics to use.

D

Half of the base incl. seam allowance

Fold

H

B

Q

I

G

B

A

B

A

P

Original size template (without
seam allowances) for accordion fold
(house 2) on page 70. The letters
indicate which fabrics to use.

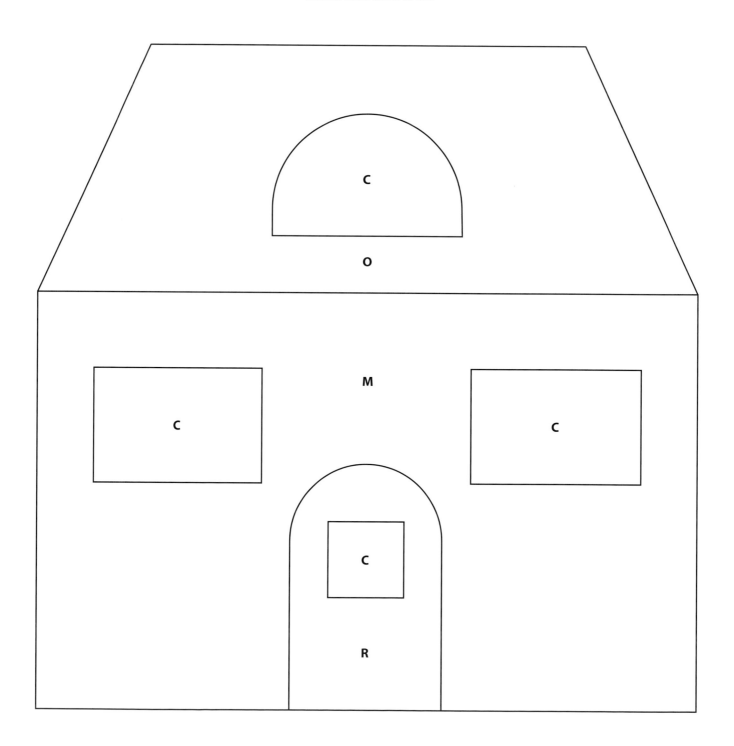

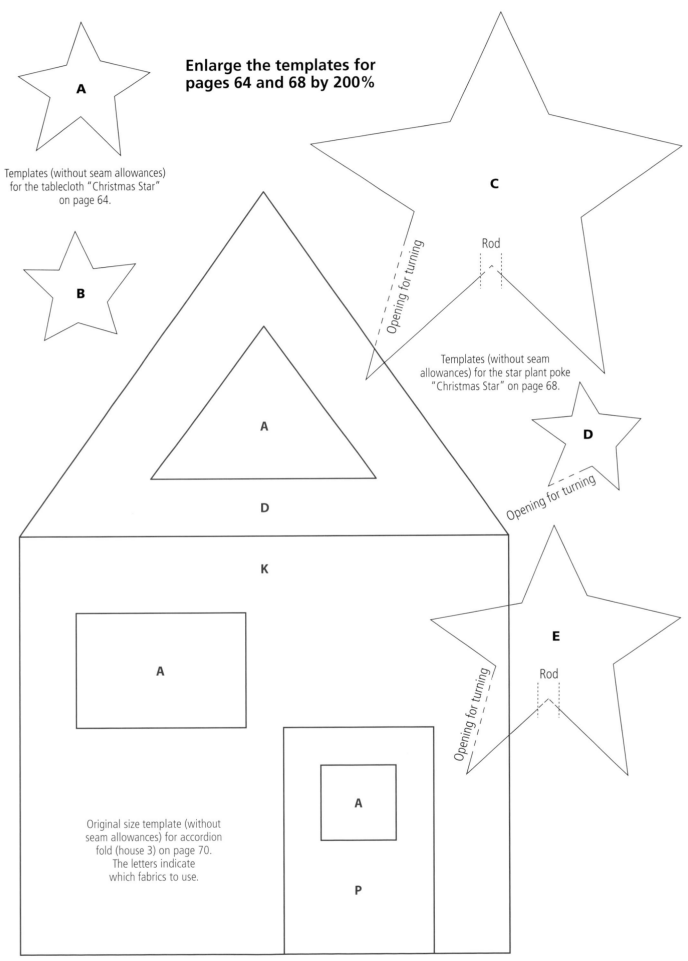

Enlarge the templates for pages 64 and 68 by 200%

A

Templates (without seam allowances) for the tablecloth "Christmas Star" on page 64.

B

C

Opening for turning

Rod

Templates (without seam allowances) for the star plant poke "Christmas Star" on page 68.

D

A

D

K

A

Opening for turning

E

Opening for turning

Rod

A

Original size template (without seam allowances) for accordion fold (house 3) on page 70. The letters indicate which fabrics to use.

P

Original size template (without seam allowances)
for accordion fold (house 4) on page 70.
The letters indicate which fabrics to use.

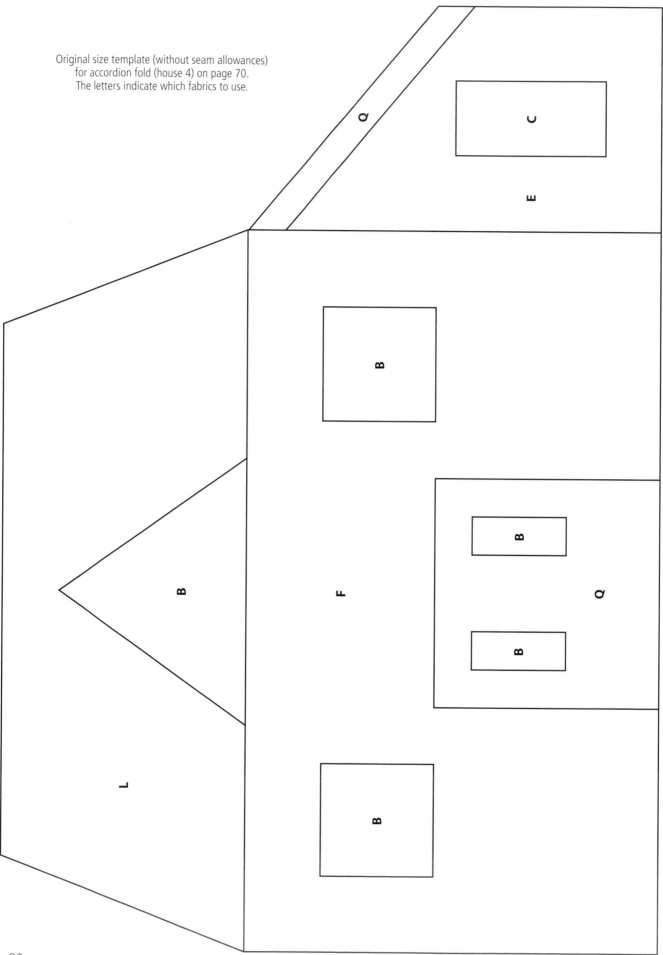

D

C

E

B

B

F

B

B

Q

L

B

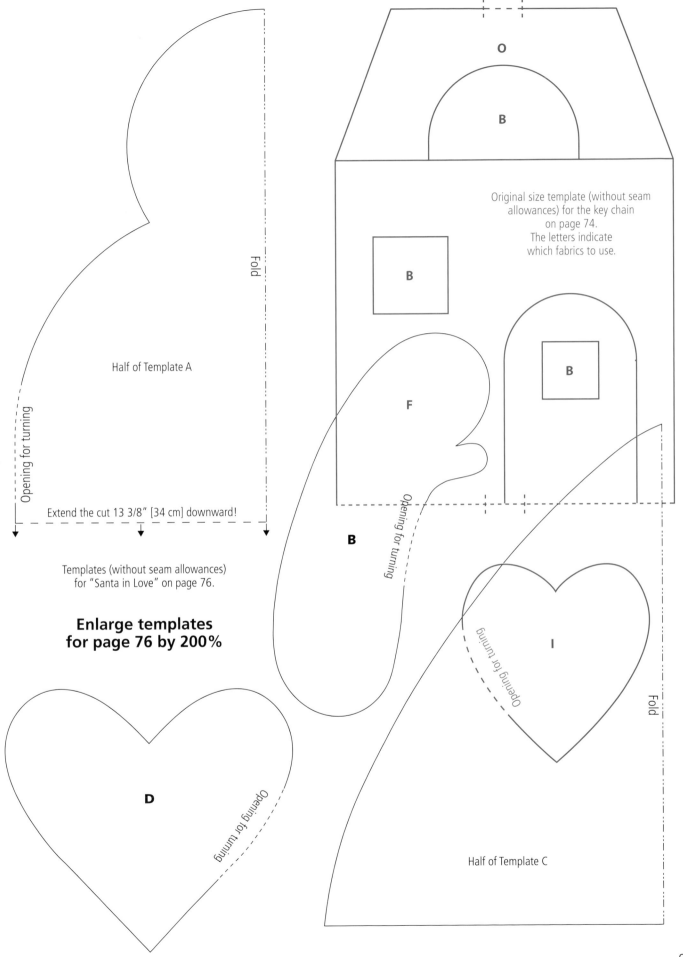

Fold

Half of Template A

Opening for turning

Extend the cut 13 3/8" [34 cm] downward!

Templates (without seam allowances)
for "Santa in Love" on page 76.

**Enlarge templates
for page 76 by 200%**

O

B

Original size template (without seam
allowances) for the key chain
on page 74.
The letters indicate
which fabrics to use.

B

B

F

Opening for turning

B

I

Opening for turning

Fold

D

Opening for turning

Half of Template C